Digital Detox for the Soul

Digital Detox for the Soul

A 21-Day Mental Cleanse

Grace Fields

Mindful Pages

Published in 2025

ISBN: 9789371346313 (PB)
ISBN: 9789371348102(eBook)

Published by

Mindful Pages
Imprint of Alpha Editions LLC
312 W. 2nd St #1834
Casper, WY 82601, USA

This book was developed using advanced writing tools to support the drafting and ideation process. All content has been thoughtfully curated, refined, and reviewed to ensure quality and relevance.

Content

Introduction
The Unseen Cost of Constant Connection

There's a curious contradiction at the heart of our hyper-connected age: never before have we been so linked, yet so inwardly fractured. We can send a message across the globe in seconds, but struggle to make contact with our own inner lives. We scroll without end, but seldom truly pause. We gather reactions in the form of likes and shares, but rarely feel truly seen. In the midst of this digital deluge, something essential seems to have slipped through our fingers—not simply time or attention, but something more elusive. Something quieter, deeper—something vital.

What if the malaise that haunts so many of us isn't just a matter of distraction, but of estrangement—from the self? What if the digital noise isn't merely an outside interference, but a static we've internalised? A hum now lodged in the nervous system, in the emotional body, even in the soul's quieter chambers. The central premise of this book is both provocative and painfully familiar: our digital habits aren't just moulding our minds—they're thinning our capacity to be whole, to be present, to feel vividly alive.

Yes, smartphones, social networks, and algorithm-driven lives offer immense utility. Few would deny the advantages. Yet these tools, powerful as they are, exact a hidden toll. It's the tension lodged between the shoulder blades. The edginess that arises in stillness. The oddly hollow fatigue that lingers after a weekend of passive leisure. Something feels off-kilter. Our bodies often register the imbalance long before the intellect catches on. This isn't an anti-tech manifesto. Rather, it's a call to recognise the sacred disarray technology has introduced—and to seek a gentler, more integrated rhythm.

We are, whether we realise it or not, entangled in an economy of attention. Fragmentation isn't incidental—it's the engine. Each ping, buzz, or alert is not simply a prompt. It's a tug—away from breath, from body, from that quiet knowing that speaks in silence. This is no accident. The systems we engage with are engineered to stir our most ancient instincts: vigilance, craving, compulsive pursuit. In bypassing our deeper human capacities—discernment, stillness, meaning—they're not just tweaking our habits. They're remapping our sense of self. Slowly. Subtly. Irrevocably.

Digital Detox for the Soul isn't offering tips for digital minimalism, nor is it another entry in the crowded field of productivity literature. It's something older, slower, and more essential. A reminder that our attention—fiercely finite and easily co-opted—is not merely a resource, but a form of reverence. This is a call not to efficiency, but to wakefulness—in its oldest, spiritual sense. To become conscious of where our attention flows, and to reckon honestly with what that flow is shaping in return.

To detox, in this context, doesn't mean fleeing to a cabin or swearing off screens. It means tending to the whole system: body, mind, soul. It means soothing a frazzled nervous system that's been locked in chronic alert. It means remembering—deep in the bones—that slowness isn't laziness, that boredom isn't failure, and that silence is not void but source. The promise is not grandiose, but it is profound: you can come back to yourself—not by adding more, but by letting go of what clutters.

Across nine chapters, this book weaves neuroscience with the durable threads of ancient wisdom. You'll trace the effects of digital immersion on stress responses and neural plasticity. You'll discover how simple, repeated acts—micro-habits, sensory rituals, breath-centred practices—can begin to shift your inner landscape. There will be reflections on silence, on meaning, on the strange gifts of boredom. And slowly, you'll learn to reclaim what is most often ceded unconsciously: your mornings, your rest, your interior spaciousness. Not through force, but through design.

What sets this work apart is its refusal to reduce the problem to dopamine or screen time. It insists on something more confronting: that what's at stake isn't only performance or peace of mind, but our very sense of soul. Our devices have infiltrated not just our calendars but our inner compass. They've altered how we measure worth, how we relate to mortality, how we encounter the rawness of feeling. This is not simply a neurological battle. It's a metaphysical one.

If you find yourself weary but unable to say why, if your mind gallops even when nothing is urgent, if you check your phone without any clear intention—or if you sense both overstimulation and emotional emptiness—you are not malfunctioning. You are responding, wisely in fact, to systems that were never built to honour human complexity. Your attention isn't broken. It's been over-extracted. Your body isn't weak. It's protesting. Your soul isn't absent. It's murmuring beneath the digital din.

This book won't urge you to forsake the world. It will ask you to move through it with greater care. It will ask you to draw firmer lines, to revere slowness, to treat attention not as currency, but as consecration. Each chapter is offered as both mirror and compass—reflecting the cost of our current entanglements, and offering pathways to something more embodied, more coherent. The goal is not escape. It's return. Not scorn, but reimagination. Not numbing, but deep, startling presence.

You'll be encouraged to linger. To breathe in ways that settle rather than stir. You'll be asked to sit with the awkwardness that arises when the dopamine runs dry—not as a sign of failure, but as the beginning of something new. That initial discomfort isn't a bug in the system—it *is* the system recalibrating. And on the far side of that discomfort lies a quiet spaciousness. For thought. For awe. For sorrow and song. A spaciousness not merely of time, but of soul.

In the end, this is not a book about technology at all. It is a meditation on sovereignty. On reclaiming the authorship of your life. Because attention is not just the means by which we move through the world. It is the medium by which the world is made. And so we arrive at the question behind every page, quiet but insistent: What will you give the weight of your attention to?

You are not here to optimise. You are here to awaken.

Let this book be a kind of Sabbath for your inner life. Let it sift and rinse and realign. Let it guide you home to what was never lost, only drowned out: presence, clarity, and the profound simplicity of feeling whole. This is no how-to manual. It is an open door.

Should you choose to walk through—not with analysis, but with your full being—the journey ahead is not merely one of detox. It is one of return.

Chapter 1
The Nervous System in the Age of Noise

There is a quiet crisis unfurling in our shared physiology—one that doesn't crash into our lives with sirens but whispers with vibrations. It doesn't shout; it pings. We don't flee from it, because we've invited it in. It sleeps beside us, nestled beneath our pillows, rests in our palms, and hums softly from our pockets. This is the slow disintegration of our nervous system's regulatory balance, gradually worn down by the persistent friction of digital stimuli. And because this erosion is both subtle and socially normalised, it rarely registers as distress. Instead, it sets the tone—a background buzz of unease, an inability to settle, and a nervous system perched constantly on the edge of alert, ready to twitch at the next nudge.

Let's not pretend the digital world we've built is neutral. It's not. It's been carefully, almost cunningly, engineered to capture and hold our attention. Notifications, breaking headlines, infinite scrolls—they're not designed merely to inform, but to provoke, to pull us in. To your nervous system, these are not trivial cues. They arrive as micro-threats, setting off the same cascades of stress that our ancestors reserved for life-or-death moments. Your heart rate flicks upward, breathing turns shallow, muscles brace—then, almost reflexively, you reach for the device, take your hit of stimulation, and move along. Do this hundreds of times a day, and the toll is no longer just psychological. It is physiological. Systemic.

Our nervous system, let's remember, is ancient. It wasn't built for this. It evolved in a world where sudden noises or flickers of motion often meant danger—predators, storms, the unexpected. In that context, immediate attention was a matter of survival. Fast-forward to now, and the same response is being hijacked by digital alerts. The threat is no longer a sabre-toothed cat but a push notification, and yet the body doesn't know the difference. It reacts all the same. Over time, the stress response becomes not occasional but habitual. Many of us are living in a near-constant state of sympathetic nervous system dominance—tense, reactive, and quietly depleted.

This chapter is a reckoning. Not a moralising account, but a clear-eyed attempt to name what's happening. Because what we often call "digital addiction" is not some personal defect. It's not a matter of willpower. It's a physiological state—an overstimulated, dysregulated nervous system reaching for balance using the very things that destabilise it. This is why abstinence alone so often fails. The solution lies not just in changing habits, but in understanding the body's deep entanglement in these behaviours. It begins with learning the nervous system's language.

Neuroscience, thankfully, does not leave us stranded. The concept of neuroplasticity—the brain's remarkable ability to rewire itself through experience—offers genuine promise. Just as our attention has been trained to scatter through dopamine hits, app toggling, and the compulsive refresh of feeds, so too can it be trained to gather, to steady. With deliberate practice, presence can be remembered. Focus restored. Stillness reclaimed—not as indulgence, but as return. Yet this restoration isn't merely cognitive. It is, at heart, embodied. The body must be brought in—not as an accessory, but as the central stage on which this transformation unfolds.

The sympathetic state—the famed "fight-or-flight" mode—has its place. It saves lives. But when activated chronically, it wears us down. It disrupts digestion, stifles creativity, interrupts sleep, and warps emotional equilibrium. What's needed is a return to the parasympathetic, the rest-and-digest mode, where healing and integration occur. But here's the catch: this shift can't be forced through another productivity hack or positive affirmation. It must be *felt*—summoned through breath, through rhythm, through sensory safety. The body needs to feel that it is safe before it can exhale.

And let's talk about multitasking—not just as a productivity myth, but as a spiritual injury. In a culture enamoured with efficiency, doing many things at once has come to signify competence. Yet the brain doesn't truly multitask; it switch-tasks. Each switch, however slight, incurs a cost: focus splinters, errors multiply, depth dissolves. But deeper still, something more sacred is lost. When we divide our attention, we dilute our presence. And when presence thins, so too does meaning.

The soul doesn't flourish in fragments. It seeks wholeness. It longs for immersion—for that unbroken thread between attention, action, and awareness. But multitasking tears at that thread. It keeps us on the surface of our own experience, skimming from task to task, rarely landing. And after enough time spent this way, the restless pace starts to feel normal. We confuse it with vitality. We chase speed as if it were purpose. What results isn't simply fatigue—it's estrangement. Estrangement from our own lives, and from the still centre within.

This chapter isn't a rejection of technology. It's an invitation to look more closely at its effects—on the brain, yes, but also on the body, the self, the texture of consciousness itself. With the help of neuroscience, physiology, and contemplative insight, we'll explore how the nervous system is both the casualty and the crucible of our digital era. You'll see how attention is hijacked, why it's so vulnerable, and how it can be reclaimed—by training the body in presence and creating environments that support regulation rather than disruption.

This is a manual for rewiring—not in metaphor, but in literal neurological terms. Through tiny practices—pausing, breathing, doing one thing at a time—we can begin to undo the effects of years of hyperstimulation. Your craving for digital input isn't irrational. It's learned. And unlearning it means turning down the noise and listening differently—to the breath, to the body, to the signals you've tuned out in favour of the scroll.

This isn't a screed against screens. It's a gesture of reverence for the nervous system. For it is here—in this responsive, ancient, quietly intelligent system—that both harm and healing reside. When we learn to read its cues, to respond with care, we recover not just attention but depth. Rhythm. Meaning.

To begin this recalibration is to admit that the issue is not simply technological. It's internal. It's in the way our muscles brace, the way our breath tightens, the way our jaw clenches without us noticing. It's in the subtle withdrawal of the soul when it senses no sanctuary. And it's in the hope that, through awareness and compassion, we might coax it back.

What follows is not a how-to. It is a map of return. A guide not to nostalgia, but to something older still—the body's innate wisdom, the mind's quiet clarity. This is a new kind of attention, one that honours its own fragility and understands its power to shape our world.

You are not broken. You are saturated. And this chapter is an opening—an invitation to reclaim your nervous system, not by fleeing the modern world, but by finding a steadier place within it.

Shall we begin?

Tech Triggers and the Hijacked Brain

You don't decide to reach for your phone—you just do. Mid-conversation, mid-task, mid-thought. Your hand moves before your mind catches up. It's a microsecond reflex, not a conscious choice. And when the screen lights up with a notification, the heart rate jumps, the pupils dilate slightly, and the body tenses—barely perceptibly, but enough to register. These are not quirks of habit. They are evidence of something far more profound: your brain has been trained, through repetition and design, to treat digital cues as urgent, attention-worthy, and potentially threatening. And that training, while invisible, is reshaping your inner world.

At the core of this phenomenon is a system designed not for modern life, but for survival in the wild: the amygdala-driven threat response. In evolutionary terms, this system was essential. It enabled our ancestors to detect danger swiftly and respond without hesitation. But in a world where most threats are symbolic, digital, or social—where the lion has been replaced by a red badge on your messaging app—the same response still fires. And it fires often.

Each notification is a variable reward—sometimes it's good news, sometimes it's a demand, sometimes it's nothing. That unpredictability activates the brain's dopaminergic system, the same circuit involved in gambling addiction. It's not the content but the *possibility* of content that keeps us checking. The scroll feed works similarly. Social media platforms, especially, exploit what behavioural scientists call "intermittent reinforcement"—a technique known to be the most habit-forming. The brain cannot predict what comes next, so it keeps pulling the lever, swiping, scrolling, refreshing, hoping the next hit will be worth it.

The cumulative effect is a nervous system in constant low-grade alert. Most people would not describe themselves as stressed when scrolling Instagram or refreshing their inbox. And yet, their bodies tell another story: increased cortisol levels, disrupted circadian rhythms, heightened muscle tension, and erratic breathing patterns. Over time, this state of near-continuous sympathetic arousal becomes the baseline. It feels *normal*, but it is profoundly corrosive.

Consider the act of multitasking, often glorified in professional and academic environments. While it may appear efficient on the surface, the neurological reality is different. The brain does not multitask; it *task switches*. Each switch imposes a cognitive tax—disrupting short-term memory, increasing error rates, and diminishing overall performance. But again, the physiological consequences are often ignored. Each switch activates a mini-stress response, as the brain must recalibrate and reorient itself repeatedly. This fragmented focus mirrors the fragmented state of the nervous system, where coherence is sacrificed for speed.

What's more, the digital environment is designed to be adversarial to attention. Tech companies employ cognitive psychologists and behavioural economists not to enhance wellbeing but to extend engagement time. The more time you spend, the more data is collected, and the more advertising revenue is generated. This is not conspiracy thinking; it is business strategy. When your attention becomes a commodity, your nervous system becomes collateral.

The ethical implications are significant. If the design of digital products actively exploits vulnerabilities in our cognitive and emotional architecture, then the impact is not just personal—it is societal. Children raised on devices are exhibiting signs of attention dysregulation earlier than ever. Adults are finding it harder to read deeply, reflect quietly, or tolerate silence. And across age groups, the result is the same: a diminished capacity for sustained presence, with all the psychological and spiritual consequences that entails.

Critically, this is not a call to demonise technology. It is a call to *understand what it's doing to us at a level most don't consider.* The issue is not the tool itself, but how it's used—and more importantly, how it's designed to be used. The hijacked brain is not a failure of discipline. It is a predictable outcome of exposure to systems engineered for compulsion. And that distinction matters. Because if the problem is framed as a lack of willpower, the solution becomes more self-control. But if the problem is neurobiological conditioning, then the solution must include *rewiring the system itself.*

So how do we begin to reverse this? Not through sheer abstinence, which often leads to rebound behaviours, but through *intentional, embodied recalibration.* It starts with recognising the cues. Notice what your body does when your phone buzzes—does your breath pause? Does your posture shift? Does your heart rate spike? That awareness alone begins to reintroduce agency. From there, we introduce pauses, interruptions in the stimulus-response loop. A breath before you check. A moment of choice inserted where there used to be automaticity.

There is also a growing body of research supporting the idea that tech-induced stress can be mitigated through sensory anchoring. Practices like grounding (touching natural surfaces), orienting (consciously scanning your environment), and conscious exhalation (elongating the out-breath) engage the parasympathetic nervous system. These are not esoteric rituals; they are physiological recalibrations—ways of signalling to the body that it is safe to return to baseline. And once safety is felt, clarity can emerge.

The philosophical layer is perhaps the most confronting. When we outsource our attentional agency to algorithms, we surrender not just time but self-authorship. We become reactive beings, shaped by the cadence of platforms rather than the rhythms of nature or inner knowing. This degrades not only cognitive sovereignty but the very conditions necessary for insight, creativity, and meaning-making. The hijacked brain is not just a neurochemical event—it is a spiritual one. It dislocates us from the present, from our bodies, and ultimately from ourselves.

To live attentively in a world engineered for distraction is not a passive condition—it is a *discipline.* And disciplines are not built overnight. They are constructed through repetition, reflection, and a willingness to value presence over novelty. This requires a revaluation of what we consider productive, meaningful, and worthy of our time. It requires saying no not just to the device, but to the internalised demand that we always be available, responsive, and updated.

What you are reclaiming is not just focus. You are reclaiming your nervous system from a state of chronic activation. You are restoring the conditions for rest, integration, and coherent attention. This is not optional. It is foundational—because a dysregulated nervous system cannot sustain clarity, intimacy, or joy. It can only chase the next thing.

The good news is that the brain remains plastic. The same circuits that were hijacked can be redirected. The habits that once reinforced stress can be repurposed to cultivate calm. But it begins with truth. With seeing the cost. With naming the pattern. With stepping out of the trance long enough to feel what has been compromised.

And that is what this chapter, and this book, aims to offer—not panic, but perspective. Not shame, but strategy. Not escape, but engagement on wiser terms. Because your attention is not a resource to be mined. It is a sacred act of creation.

What you give it to, you strengthen. What you strengthen, you become. The question is no longer whether your brain is being shaped. It is—daily. The question is: *by whom, and toward what end?*

Neuroplasticity and the Art of Inner Rewiring

The brain you are using to read this sentence is not the same brain you woke up with this morning. It has changed—not drastically, not dramatically, but subtly, silently, and inevitably. Every thought, every scroll, every repeated habit has left a trace. This is not philosophy; it is biology. The human brain is not fixed but plastic—an organ in constant dialogue with experience. And while this adaptability is our evolutionary gift, it is also our modern vulnerability. For what we repeat, we reinforce. And in a digital culture that thrives on compulsion and fragmentation, our neuroplasticity is being spent, often unconsciously, on habits that diminish rather than deepen our capacity for presence.

Neuroplasticity—the brain's ability to reorganise itself by forming new neural connections throughout life—is one of the most significant scientific discoveries of the last century. It overturned centuries of belief that the brain, like a finished sculpture, solidified with age. We now understand that the brain remains dynamic, responsive, and exquisitely sensitive to repeated input. This is good news—provided we are mindful of what we are repeating.

The modern digital environment, however, is not neutral. It is designed to capture attention, interrupt thought, and trigger habitual engagement. Each time you reach for your device during a lull in conversation, while waiting in a queue, or during the first stirrings of boredom, you are not just relieving discomfort—you are strengthening a neural pathway. Over time, this pathway becomes a preference, and preference becomes compulsion. The brain, trained by repetition, begins to crave stimulation not for its content, but for its predictability. What begins as convenience becomes conditioning.

Studies in cognitive neuroscience have shown that the default mode network (DMN)—the brain's system for introspection, daydreaming, and self-referential thought—activates during periods of rest and non-engagement. But when we compulsively fill every idle moment with digital input, the DMN is starved of oxygen. We lose the natural rhythm between external interaction and internal integration. This has far-reaching consequences, not only for memory consolidation and emotional processing but for our very sense of continuity. Without regular access to stillness, the self becomes scattered—overstimulated, yet under-reflected.

This matters because the brain's plasticity does not discriminate. It will adapt to whatever is rehearsed—whether that rehearsal serves our flourishing or not. Attention span, impulse control, emotional regulation, even compassion—these are not fixed traits, but malleable skills. They strengthen with use. Or they atrophy with neglect. In this light, digital overwhelm is not merely an inconvenience. It is a form of self-shaping we may not have consented to but are nonetheless participating in.

The ethical dimension here is worth noting. If our neural architecture is being altered by platforms engineered for engagement rather than wellbeing, then the question is not just scientific but philosophical: *What are we allowing our minds to become, and who benefits from that transformation?* This is not a call for paranoia. It is a call for responsibility. For while we cannot control the existence of persuasive technologies, we can reclaim authorship over our internal landscapes.

Intentional rituals are one such act of authorship. They are not nostalgic returns to simpler times, but strategic responses to the neurobiological demands of modern life. Unlike fleeting resolutions or productivity tools, rituals work by engaging the nervous system directly. They provide reliable cues, structured repetition, and embodied coherence—all essential ingredients for rewiring. A morning breath practice, for instance, becomes more than a wellness trend. It is a neuroplastic intervention—a way of reintroducing rhythm, depth, and predictability into a day shaped by digital entropy.

Rituals also speak to the limbic brain—the emotional and relational core of the nervous system. Where analytical tools rely on executive function, rituals tap into felt memory and symbolic continuity. Lighting a candle before journaling, stretching before bed, walking without headphones—these are not quaint habits but acts of neural stewardship. They tell the brain: *this moment is different, deliberate, and worth remembering*. And repetition transforms them from novelty into structure, from effort into ease.

The science supports this. Researchers at UCLA and MIT have shown that habit formation involves a shift from goal-directed action to automaticity via the basal ganglia, a deep brain structure responsible for procedural learning. But this shift requires consistency, minimal cognitive load, and emotional salience—all of which are cultivated through well-designed rituals. In other words, we do not need more willpower. We need fewer decisions, more rhythm, and rituals that align with the states we wish to inhabit.

Contrast this with the prevailing model of behaviour change, which often centres on discipline and denial. We are told to resist, abstain, and uninstall. But neuroscience suggests that the brain responds far more reliably to replacement than to restriction. If we want to spend less time on our phones, we must ask: *What will we do instead?* And more importantly, *how can that alternative be made more emotionally rewarding, physiologically soothing, and neurologically reinforcing?*

This is where the art of inner rewiring begins. It is not about fighting the old pattern, but about establishing a new one that is more compelling. A pattern that meets the nervous system not with deprivation but with regulation. This could be as simple as inserting a pause before checking your phone, during which you take three conscious breaths and notice your surroundings. It could be a midday moment of silence, cued by the closing of a laptop. These are not hacks; they are neural doorways—small, repeatable actions that create conditions for larger shifts in perception and behaviour.

But ritual alone is not enough. What gives it power is intentionality. Neuroplasticity is enhanced by what scientists call "attention density"—the depth and frequency with which we bring focused awareness to an experience. Mindless repetition may form habits, but mindful repetition rewires identity. When we approach a practice not as a means to an end but as an act of care, the brain encodes it differently. It becomes meaningful. And meaning, as Viktor Frankl and contemporary neuroscientists alike have observed, is one of the most potent forces in shaping neural architecture.

There are tensions to navigate, of course. Some critics argue that the emphasis on personal rewiring risks privatising what are, in part, systemic problems. And there is truth in that concern. No amount of meditation can undo the exploitative attention economy. But this is not an either/or proposition. Individual sovereignty and systemic reform must proceed in parallel. One does not excuse the other. If anything, a regulated nervous system is better equipped to resist, critique, and innovate within broken systems. And that is the deeper promise of neuroplasticity—not just personal tranquillity, but collective clarity.

To rewire is to remember that we are not passive recipients of technological conditioning. We are, at every moment, co-authors of our inner lives. And that authorship begins with noticing. With choosing. With repeating. Not mechanically, but reverently. The brain, after all, is always listening. The question is: *what message are we sending it through our rituals, our rhythms, and our repeated attention?*

You are not stuck with the mind that culture has shaped for you. You can reshape it—slowly, deliberately, and with care. The path back to presence is not a sprint. It is a sequence of small, sacred repetitions. And in their quiet regularity lies the power to become someone new—not by escaping the world, but by becoming more awake within it.

From Fight-or-Flight to Rest-and-Repair

Stress has become so ubiquitous in modern life that many people no longer recognise its presence—only its consequences. Sleep that never quite restores, fatigue that caffeine can't cure, irritability that masquerades as urgency. We tell ourselves we're just busy, just tired, just going through a rough patch. But behind these surface symptoms lies a deeper physiological reality: the human body is stuck in a state of chronic sympathetic overdrive. And unless we understand the mechanisms of that state—what activates it, what sustains it, and crucially, what can unwind it—we remain at the mercy of a system that was never designed for constant activation.

The autonomic nervous system is the body's master regulator. It operates below the level of conscious awareness, overseeing vital functions such as heart rate, digestion, respiration, and immune response. This system is composed of two primary branches: the sympathetic nervous system (SNS), which mobilises the body for action, and the parasympathetic nervous system (PNS), which restores it to rest. These two systems are not in opposition but in dynamic balance—ideally alternating like the in-breath and out-breath, tension and release.

The problem is not the existence of the fight-or-flight response. That response is vital. It readies the body to respond to real danger. The issue is its chronic activation in environments that are not dangerous, but *demanding*. Notifications, deadlines, social media feedback loops, financial pressure, information overload—each one triggers a low-grade stress response. Not enough to make you bolt from the room, but enough to elevate cortisol, suppress digestion, and subtly prime the body for conflict or escape. Over time, this creates a physiological feedback loop: the more the SNS is activated, the more it stays activated. And the more it stays activated, the harder it becomes to access the PNS and its life-sustaining benefits.

One of the most misunderstood aspects of stress is its invisibility. Acute stress—the kind triggered by a sudden loud noise or a confrontation—registers clearly. We feel the spike. But chronic stress operates more like a background hum. It becomes the new normal. And because it is subtle, we adapt to it rather than address it. We drink more coffee, sleep less deeply, become more reactive and less resilient. But the body keeps the score. And the tally is steep: inflammation, hormonal dysregulation, cardiovascular strain, cognitive fog, and emotional volatility.

To reverse this pattern requires more than relaxation. It requires *regulation.* Relaxation is passive; regulation is active. It involves cultivating physiological states that send clear signals to the brain: *you are safe now; you can let go.* This is the territory of the parasympathetic nervous system, particularly the ventral branch of the vagus nerve, which governs states of calm, connection, and homeostasis. Engaging this system is not about numbing or zoning out. It is about shifting into a state where healing, digestion, immune function, and emotional integration can occur.

One of the most reliable ways to engage the PNS is through the breath. But not just any breath. Fast, shallow breathing—especially through the mouth—can actually reinforce sympathetic activation. What we need is slow, diaphragmatic breathing, ideally with an extended exhalation. Research from institutions like Stanford and the HeartMath Institute has shown that a prolonged out-breath stimulates the vagus nerve, signalling the body to downregulate. Even a few minutes a day of conscious breathing—say, inhaling for four counts, exhaling for six—can begin to shift the body out of emergency mode and into rest-and-repair.

Movement also plays a role, but the kind of movement matters. High-intensity workouts, while beneficial in moderation, can sometimes mimic the stress response if layered on top of an already taxed system. Gentle, rhythmic movement—such as walking, yoga, or tai chi—tends to be more effective for rebalancing the nervous system. These activities combine breath, rhythm, and embodiment, all of which help the system return to baseline.

Touch is another powerful regulator. Human beings are wired for contact. Even light pressure on the skin can stimulate parasympathetic activity. This is why practices like self-massage, weighted blankets, or simply placing a hand over the heart can be unexpectedly effective. It's not mystical—it's neurobiological. The skin, especially around the chest and abdomen, is rich with mechanoreceptors that communicate directly with the nervous system. When these are activated gently, the body reads the signal: *no danger here.*

Sleep, of course, is the body's most potent restorative state. But for many people caught in sympathetic dominance, sleep becomes elusive. They lie down, but the mind races. They wake up feeling unrefreshed. What's happening is that the body has not received the signal that it's safe to drop into deep rest. This is why pre-sleep rituals—dim lights, no screens, gentle stretching, even consistent bedtime routines—are not indulgences. They are neurological cues that help transition the body from activation to surrender. They matter not because they are relaxing, but because they are regulatory.

It's important to note that transitioning from sympathetic overdrive to parasympathetic healing is not a binary switch. It's a spectrum. And movement along that spectrum is not always linear. There are days when the system will resist, when old habits pull hard, when external stressors overwhelm internal resources. This is not failure. It is part of the recalibration process. What matters is not perfection, but patterning—establishing enough repetition of healing signals that the body begins to expect, and eventually prefer, states of calm.

There are also social dimensions to consider. The parasympathetic state is not just about solitude and quiet. It is also deeply relational. The presence of safe others—people with whom we feel seen, heard, and understood—can be one of the most powerful regulators. The pioneering work of Dr Stephen Porges in Polyvagal Theory highlights this, showing how facial expression, vocal tone, and eye contact contribute to what he calls *neuroception of safety.* In other words, our nervous system is constantly scanning our environment, not just for threats, but for signs of support. When it finds them, it relaxes. This is why healthy social connection is not a luxury—it is a neural necessity.

Yet many of us have internalised a culture that equates productivity with worth and stillness with sloth. We live under what some scholars call *stress normalisation*—the idea that being constantly busy, hyper-reactive, and under pressure is just part of being a functioning adult. But this is a cultural pathology, not a biological imperative. The human body is not built for relentless acceleration. It is built for rhythm. For cycles. For alternating states of exertion and restoration. To ignore this is not just to court burnout—it is to erode the very systems that support cognition, immunity, intimacy, and creativity.

The shift from fight-or-flight to rest-and-repair, then, is not only physiological—it is philosophical. It asks us to question the values and narratives that keep us in overdrive. It asks us to create spaces—physical, temporal, and psychological—where slowness is not a deviation from purpose but a return to it. It asks us to see rest not as the absence of doing, but as the foundation of being.

Ultimately, healing the nervous system is not a self-improvement project. It is a reclamation of something innate—an intelligence that has never been lost, only overridden. The body knows how to rest. The nervous system knows how to heal. Our task is not to force it, but to create the conditions under which that healing becomes possible again. We do this through breath, through ritual, through attention, through love.

And most of all, through the courage to slow down—not because we are weak, but because we are wise enough to remember that life, like the body, thrives in rhythm. And in that rhythm, healing begins.

Digital Addiction Is a Nervous System Issue

The term *addiction* is often lobbed carelessly in conversations about technology—used to describe everything from compulsive scrolling to the urge to check a device within seconds of waking. It's a word that carries weight, frequently shadowed by judgement, stigma, and a reductive assumption: that the individual simply lacks discipline. But when we look more closely—at the neurological patterns, the physiological feedback loops, and the psychological underpinnings—a different picture emerges. What we label "digital addiction" is less a failure of willpower than a state of *nervous system dysregulation.* It is not fundamentally a behavioural flaw; it is a biological adaptation gone awry.

To understand this, we must begin with the human stress response. The autonomic nervous system governs our capacity to respond to stress and regulate emotion. It is split into two core branches: the sympathetic nervous system, which readies the body for action (fight-or-flight), and the parasympathetic nervous system, which facilitates rest, repair, and connection. This system is exquisitely responsive to perceived safety or threat—not just physical, but emotional and environmental. And in a culture of chronic stimulation, uncertainty, and pressure, many people live in a near-constant state of sympathetic activation. Their bodies remain subtly braced, hyper-vigilant, and unable to fully settle.

Enter the digital device: not as a neutral tool, but as a self-soothing mechanism. When the nervous system feels dysregulated—anxious, overwhelmed, fatigued—the impulse is to seek regulation. And digital technologies offer exactly that, at least superficially. The screen delivers predictable rewards, micro-doses of stimulation, and a temporary sense of control or distraction. In the language of neuroscience, this is classic *dopaminergic reinforcement.* But rather than resolving the dysregulation, it compounds it—creating a cycle in which the system becomes increasingly reliant on external stimulation to feel balanced, while losing the ability to self-regulate from within.

Consider a common scenario: you've had a difficult conversation, your heart rate is elevated, and your thoughts are looping. Instead of pausing to breathe, move, or process, you reach for your phone. A few swipes through social media or messages provide momentary relief. Your body calms—not because the underlying tension has been addressed, but because the attention has been redirected.

You've distracted the stress signal rather than resolved it. Over time, this strategy becomes automatic. The phone becomes the pacifier. The nervous system, never given space to complete its stress response, remains stuck in partial activation.

This is why it is misleading to treat digital overuse as a simple matter of habit. Habits can be changed through effort and planning. But *patterns of dysregulation require nervous system repair*. The addicted state is not the presence of weakness—it is the absence of internal safety. And until that safety is re-established physiologically, attempts at digital detox often fail or backfire. People uninstall apps, turn off notifications, or declare screen-free weekends, only to find themselves agitated, bored, or emotionally raw within hours. What they're experiencing is not withdrawal—it's the unveiling of unprocessed nervous system states that the device had been masking.

It's important to differentiate between different kinds of compulsive use. Some behaviours are purely reward-seeking—checking for likes, obsessing over metrics, chasing novelty. Others are more defensive—using the screen to avoid social discomfort, emotional overwhelm, or existential unease. In both cases, the behaviour serves a regulatory function. And so, any meaningful intervention must include nervous system regulation as a foundational component—not just a behavioural change, but a *somatic recalibration*.

Emerging research in trauma science offers useful insights here. The work of pioneers like Dr Stephen Porges (Polyvagal Theory) and Dr Bessel van der Kolk (*The Body Keeps the Score*) has shown that the nervous system's response to threat is deeply embedded and often unconscious. It does not rely on rational analysis; it relies on felt experience. If the body does not feel safe—regardless of the actual risk—it will seek regulation through the fastest, most accessible means. And for many, that means their device.

This shifts the conversation from blame to biology. Instead of asking, "Why can't I stop checking my phone?" a more productive question might be: "What state is my nervous system in when I reach for it?" This invites curiosity over criticism. It also opens the door to targeted practices that work with, rather than against, the body's stress-response architecture.

For example, breathwork is not just calming—it is regulating. Slow, nasal breathing with elongated exhales activates the vagus nerve, signalling the body to downshift. Similarly, grounding techniques—such as orienting to the room, feeling the weight of your body, or using sensory anchors like touch or sound—help restore the nervous system's sense of situational safety. These practices don't eliminate the impulse to check a device, but they reduce its urgency. They widen the window of choice.

Yet there's another layer here, more existential in nature. Devices don't just soothe the nervous system—they also help us avoid ourselves. The screen offers a portal away from discomfort: emotional, relational, even spiritual. In this light, digital addiction becomes not just a nervous system issue, but a crisis of inner presence. We lose tolerance for boredom, uncertainty, slowness, even joy. We become conditioned to stimulation as the baseline of being. And when life doesn't provide it, we seek it artificially. This is not just about the brain—it's about our relationship to aliveness.

This has implications not only for personal health but for cultural ethics. When a society normalises overuse of devices, it also normalises dysregulation. Workplaces reward constant connectivity, educational systems digitise increasingly early, and social norms favour availability over autonomy. In such an environment, the individual's nervous system is perpetually taxed. To resist this is not indulgent—it is an act of care, of sovereignty, and ultimately, of resistance against a model of attention that prioritises efficiency over humanity.

Critics may argue that the language of addiction is exaggerated, or that nervous system framing risks medicalising what is essentially behavioural. But this critique often misses the core insight: that *behaviour is downstream of regulation.* You cannot sustainably change what you habitually do until you repair the conditions in which you are doing it. This is why cognitive strategies alone—setting timers, using willpower, downloading monitoring apps—so often fail. They address the symptom, not the system.

A more integrated approach must begin with awareness. Track not just *how often* you use your device, but *what state* you're in before and after. Begin to notice the cues—tightness in the chest, shallow breathing, restlessness in the hands. Then, instead of suppressing these sensations with a scroll, practise staying. Name what's present. Breathe through it. Move. Shake. Lie on the floor. Touch your skin. Whisper something kind. Let the nervous system complete its cycle.

This is not a rejection of technology. It is a reorientation to our own biology. It is an invitation to learn the language of the body—not through theories, but through repeated, gentle contact. It is not glamorous, and it won't make headlines. But it is *foundational.* Because the capacity to be with ourselves—to feel without fleeing, to pause without panic—is the soil from which all digital discernment grows.

And from that soil, we can begin to rebuild a life where attention is not siphoned reactively, but offered deliberately. Where the phone becomes a tool, not a tether. Where the nervous system, once misregulated and seeking refuge, becomes a sanctuary. Not because we finally found the perfect app blocker, but because we returned to something deeper: the body's innate ability to settle, to feel, and to be.

Digital addiction, then, is not about too much screen time. It's about *too little inner time.* The screen is the symptom. The system is the story. And the nervous system—our oldest and most faithful guide—is ready to be listened to again.

The Myth of Multitasking and the Soul's Fragmentation

The modern mind wears multitasking like a badge of honour. "I'm juggling five projects." "I take meetings while answering emails." "I listen to podcasts at double speed while doing my workout." This fragmented engagement is often portrayed as efficiency, as a signal of competence or ambition. But beneath the surface performance lies a neurological truth that's difficult to ignore: the brain does not multitask. It switches. And every switch comes at a cost—not just to productivity, but to presence, coherence, and what could only be described as the *sacredness* of undivided attention.

Let's be precise. When people claim to multitask, what they're usually doing is *task switching*. Instead of performing two cognitive tasks simultaneously, the brain toggles rapidly between them, engaging distinct neural circuits with each shift. This phenomenon has been extensively studied in cognitive neuroscience. Research from Stanford, MIT, and the University of London consistently shows that multitasking reduces the efficiency and quality of performance in every domain. Task switching increases the likelihood of errors, delays response times, and impairs working memory. Far from being a productivity hack, multitasking is a bandwidth tax. But what's often overlooked is that this isn't merely a technical inefficiency. It's a *spiritual and psychological fracture.*

Every time we divide our attention, we dilute our capacity to be present. And presence is not just a mental state—it is a form of intimacy with reality. When we are fully engaged in a task, a conversation, or a moment, there is a sense of coherence—a merging of thought, action, and awareness. This coherence is not trivial. It is the foundation of meaning. It's why a slow meal, a deep conversation, or a moment of stillness can feel inexplicably nourishing. It's not the content—it's the *undividedness* that restores us.

By contrast, multitasking creates an internal dissonance. We're physically here, mentally there, emotionally nowhere. The mind becomes a fragmented feed—part email, part memory, part anxiety loop. And while each fragment seems harmless in isolation, the cumulative effect is one of disintegration. We lose the thread of our own experience. And when we live this way habitually, we begin to normalise fragmentation as the texture of everyday life. Our attention becomes thin, brittle, constantly on the edge of redirection. What we don't realise is that this fragility seeps into everything: how we listen, how we relate, how we think, how we feel.

There is a reason spiritual traditions across cultures emphasise single-pointed focus. Whether it's through prayer, meditation, ritual, or craft, the act of *doing one thing fully* has long been understood as a gateway to presence, clarity, and even transcendence. Not because the activity itself is sacred, but because *our attention makes it so*. In this light, multitasking is not just a neurological strain—it is a spiritual dislocation. It prevents depth. It flattens nuance. It strips daily life of its contemplative potential.

And yet, the culture rewards this dislocation. The workplace glorifies responsiveness over thoughtfulness. Schools push for performance over presence. Social platforms reward reactivity over reflection. Multitasking becomes embedded not just as a habit but as a *social signal*—a way to demonstrate busyness, relevance, or success. But this is a profound misalignment. Because the soul does not thrive in fragments. It thrives in rhythm, in depth, in unbroken lines of attention that allow meaning to emerge.

This is not a call to retreat from complexity or live like a monk. It's a call to recognise the hidden costs of fragmentation—not in abstract philosophical terms, but in lived experience. When you eat while watching a screen, do you actually *taste* your food? When you half-listen to a loved one while checking your phone, do you *feel* their presence? When you skim five tabs open in your browser, do you *understand* any of them deeply? Multitasking doesn't just make us less efficient. It makes us less *available*—to others, to ourselves, to life as it unfolds.

There are also neurobiological consequences. Chronic multitasking has been linked with increased production of cortisol and adrenaline—stress hormones that, over time, erode our capacity for focused attention. The prefrontal cortex, responsible for executive function and decision-making, becomes overwhelmed. The default mode network, which supports reflection and self-awareness, becomes harder to access. The result is not just cognitive fatigue—it's a kind of existential flatness. We begin to feel unanchored, unable to settle, constantly pulled towards the next stimulus, the next input, the next tab.

Contrast this with *flow states*—those rare but transformative moments when we are wholly immersed in a task. Flow is not achieved by doing more, but by *doing one thing deeply.* The parameters of flow are well-documented: clear goals, immediate feedback, full absorption. In flow, time dilates, self-consciousness diminishes, and performance peaks. But more than that, *wellbeing increases.* The nervous system moves out of survival mode into coherence. There is a felt sense of alignment between intention, action, and awareness. And this is not reserved for elite performers. It is accessible to anyone willing to protect the sanctity of undivided attention.

So why don't we do it more often? Because the external world is not designed for single-tasking. It's designed for *attention extraction.* Every app, every notification, every algorithm is a bid for your cognitive resources. And if we don't create boundaries—psychological and practical—we are swept into a mode of perpetual partial attention. The answer is not simply to try harder. It is to *design your environment to support focus.* To close tabs. To turn off push notifications. To batch tasks. To treat time not as a slot to be filled, but as a container to be *honoured.*

But even that is not enough. We must go deeper, asking not just *how* we use attention, but *why.* What are we afraid of in the stillness? What discomfort are we masking with constant task-switching? What part of ourselves do we lose when we're never fully *in* anything? These are not productivity questions. They are existential ones. Because in the end, attention is not just a tool—it is the medium through which we *encounter life*. Fragment it, and life feels fragmented. Gather it, and meaning reappears.

Multitasking, then, is not merely inefficient—it is disintegrative. It trains us to be everywhere and nowhere at once. And while we may accomplish more, we *experience* less. The price of divided attention is not only cognitive—it is emotional, relational, spiritual. We feel less connected to our work, our people, our own sense of being. We begin to live *on the surface*—faster, busier, but emptier.

To live differently is not to become ascetic. It is to choose *wholeness over dispersion*, *depth over speed*, *presence over productivity theatre*. It is to reclaim attention not as a scarce commodity but as a sacred act. Not because it makes us more efficient, but because it *makes us more human*. And perhaps more than anything, it is to remember that what we do with our attention is what we do with our lives.

And that nothing truly sacred—whether a conversation, a thought, or a moment—can survive in fragments.

Chapter 2
Boredom Is the Portal

Boredom, for all its quiet persistence, has acquired a reputation it does not deserve. In contemporary culture, the word itself lands with a faint sting of judgement. To be bored is to be unmotivated, uninspired—perhaps even lazy. It implies that something vital is missing, or that we ourselves are lacking. In response, we flee it—numb it, scroll it away, silence it with sound or stimulation. But here's the paradox: boredom isn't the problem. If anything, it's a signpost—an invitation. What we interpret as discomfort is often the nervous system attempting to recalibrate, to signal that it's had quite enough noise for now.

That tug of restlessness we experience when boredom sets in? It's not failure; it's the beginning of something older and wiser stirring beneath the static. Our nervous system, dulled by overexposure to novelty and micro-rewards, is seeking something it no longer knows how to find easily: spaciousness. And because our conditioning has taught us to equate satisfaction with stimulation, we miss the message entirely. Boredom, then, isn't a void to be eliminated. It's a passage. And on the other side of that threshold lies not desolation, but potential.

Consider this chapter a quiet rebellion—an attempt to reframe boredom not as the enemy of meaning but as its peculiar guardian. First, though, we have to acknowledge a difficult truth: our culture is increasingly allergic to stillness. Silence unsettles us. Waiting seems wasteful. Slowness is viewed as a flaw. We've commodified attention to such a degree that its spiritual dimensions—its sacred potential—have all but vanished. Yet attention, in its essence, is not just a tool for getting things done. It's an act of being. What we choose to attend to shapes not only our thoughts but our character. Attention is ethical. It's a form of reverence.

When we compulsively fill each idle moment with distraction, we don't just consume—we dilute our own presence. We surrender the space in which consciousness used to unfold naturally. What was once a realm for quiet rumination or daydreaming has become a dumping ground for content. The result? A mind that collects, but does not digest. That hoards, but does not integrate. And integration, let us not forget, is the soil from which insight and coherence grow.

From a neurological standpoint, the implications are far from trivial. The brain is fundamentally a pattern-seeking organ. It thrives on anticipation and novelty—dopamine is the fuel behind much of our motivation and attention. But this system, elegant as it is, was never meant to run continuously on artificial stimulation. When bombarded with short bursts of novelty—alerts, videos, rapid scrolls—we hypercharge the brain's reward circuitry. The cost? We lose sensitivity to nuance. Our tolerance for ambiguity shrinks. Delayed gratification becomes harder to bear. In effect, boredom becomes not the absence of interest, but the symptom of a system running on empty.

This is the bind of our dopamine-saturated environment: it promises delight, but leaves us depleted. And the more we chase stimulation, the duller our receptors become to the more subtle textures of experience—those slow, rewarding currents that arise not from speed, but from depth. The satisfaction of finishing a long novel, mastering a skill, or simply watching light move across a wall—these things nourish us. They endure. But only if we can tolerate the initial quiet they require.

To be clear, this is not a call to renounce all pleasure or novelty. It's an argument for building a capacity for boredom—not as punishment, but as practice. Because when we stop fleeing from it, boredom begins to unfold. At first, yes, there may be agitation or a flicker of melancholy. But stay long enough, and something shifts. The mind, no longer chasing the next hit, starts to look inward. What it finds there is often unexpected: half-formed ideas, buried emotions, dormant creativity. What was discomfort becomes compost.

The evidence backs this up. Psychological research has shown that so-called "idle" mental time—what occurs when we are not focused on a specific task—activates the brain's default mode network. It is here that synthesis happens. New connections are made, old experiences reconfigured. This is why breakthroughs arrive unbidden—in the shower, on a walk, while staring into the middle distance. Creativity isn't always summoned by force. Sometimes, it requires us to loosen our grip.

But to allow this to happen, we have to make peace with the awkwardness that often comes first. Like any withdrawal, the early moments of unplugging can be uncomfortable. The body fidgets. The mind complains. The world feels a touch flat. But this isn't failure. It's transition. What's really happening is a subtle recalibration: the nervous system adjusting to the absence of its usual crutches. And if we can remain present through this awkward in-between, the benefits begin to appear—not as fireworks, but as a quiet returning.

This reorientation has broader implications than personal well-being. In workplaces, which are increasingly driven by metrics and immediate outputs, carving space for mental idleness can feel almost subversive. In education, boredom is often pathologised—as if a child's wandering attention is a problem to be fixed rather than a signal of deeper developmental processes. Even in our everyday lives, moments of pause—gazing out a window, sipping tea without a screen—can feel almost illicit. But perhaps these moments are not luxuries. Perhaps they're rituals of return.

Return to what, exactly? To an undivided self. To breath and texture. To presence, unmediated and unperformed. This isn't about detaching from the world—it's about re-entering it more fully, with attention that is whole rather than fractured. For when we stop chasing novelty and allow ourselves to feel boredom fully, something strange happens. We begin to listen again—to our thoughts, yes, but also to the more subtle currents of intuition and emotion that live beneath the noise. This kind of listening gives rise to a deeper knowing—an intelligence that is less about data and more about alignment.

Within this chapter, we'll trace the contours of what it means to do nothing—not as idleness, but as a mode of embodied attention. We'll dismantle the myths that equate stillness with sloth, and activity with virtue. We'll examine how the brain's reward systems are manipulated by digital design, and why that matters. We'll explore boredom as both a symptom of overstimulation and a doorway to inner life. And we'll reclaim the wandering mind—not as broken, but as beautifully alive.

What we're after, in the end, is a rewilding of attention. Letting it meander again, without leash or timeline. Letting it grow wild edges and quiet depths. Because if attention is a kind of love, then boredom is perhaps its most honest form—the place we arrive when all performance ceases. Not because we've given up, but because we've finally stopped running.

And in that stillness, something waits—something real, and utterly human.

The Lost Art of Doing Nothing

Doing nothing should be the easiest thing in the world. It demands no effort, no tools, no schedule. And yet, for many in the modern world, it is among the hardest states to enter—let alone sustain. Within seconds of stillness, there's a twitch of discomfort, a reflex to fill the gap: reach for the phone, check a screen, tidy the desk, open a new tab. The space where nothing should be quickly becomes something. This resistance is not trivial. It reveals something deeper about our conditioning: *we have pathologised stillness*. In doing so, we've severed a vital connection to one of the most generative states of the human mind.

Historically, periods of inactivity were not seen as idleness but as essential. Philosophers and spiritual teachers—from the Stoics to the mystics, from Confucian scholars to monastic traditions—understood that contemplation requires empty space. The mind, they knew, is not designed to be constantly occupied. It needs time to integrate, reflect, and metabolise experience. Today, however, the cultural narrative has reversed. Productivity has become the default metric of worth. To be busy is to be useful. To be still is to be irrelevant. But this metric is based on a dangerously narrow view of human function—one that privileges output over awareness, and activity over insight.

Neurologically, the effects of this are well documented. When we allow ourselves to do nothing—truly nothing, with no agenda or stimulation—the brain doesn't power down. It switches into a different mode: the default mode network (DMN). This network is responsible for introspection, memory consolidation, emotional processing, and creative incubation. It is during these periods that the mind sifts through unresolved experiences, makes unexpected connections, and retrieves dormant insights. In other words, *doing nothing is not the absence of function—it is the precondition for integration.*

Yet we resist it. Not because we're lazy, but because we're addicted to stimulation. The modern environment is structured around attention capture. Everything from social media to productivity apps is designed to engage, reward, and escalate. The result is that our baseline level of stimulation has increased dramatically. When that level drops—as it does in boredom or stillness—the nervous system reacts not with relief but with discomfort. This is not a moral failing. It is a neuroadaptive response. The brain, accustomed to constant input, experiences its absence as a problem to be solved.

This has profound implications for wellbeing. Without regular intervals of rest—true rest, not distracted leisure—the nervous system becomes dysregulated. Cortisol remains elevated. The body stays in a mild but persistent state of alert. The mind, unable to slow down, begins to interpret even minor silence as an existential threat. This is why many people experience anxiety when doing nothing. It's not the stillness that's dangerous; it's what the stillness reveals. Unprocessed emotions. Unmetabolised grief. Questions we've buried. But avoidance is not resolution. It is delay. And what we resist tends to resurface—more urgently and less coherently.

The challenge, then, is not just to accept stillness, but to *retrain ourselves to inhabit it.* This begins with acknowledging that the discomfort of boredom is not a problem to fix—it is a signal that the system is recalibrating. It's a detox response. The same way the body reacts when withdrawing from sugar or caffeine, the mind resists the drop in stimulation. But if we can stay with that discomfort—without reaching for a distraction—it begins to shift. We become more attuned to subtleties: the sound of breath, the texture of light, the contours of thought. The nervous system softens. The mind widens. And in that widening, something opens.

Creativity thrives here—not the forced kind born from deadlines, but the emergent kind that bubbles up from nowhere in particular. Studies have shown that people who allow time for boredom perform better on creative problem-solving tasks. Why? Because boredom invites the mind to wander. And in wandering, it encounters ideas that structured thinking often misses. The linear gives way to the lateral. The obvious gives way to the original. This is why so many artists, scientists, and thinkers report their best ideas coming during walks, showers, or long, empty afternoons.

But the benefits are not limited to creativity. Emotional processing also requires spaciousness. When we're constantly distracted, difficult emotions get deferred. We feel the edge of sadness or irritation but scroll past it. We don't sit with it, name it, or understand it. Over time, these unfelt emotions accumulate, creating a background hum of unrest. Doing nothing gives them room to surface—gently, organically. And when they do, we can meet them with attention rather than avoidance. This is not indulgence. It is integration. Emotional resilience is not the absence of emotion but the capacity to stay present with it.

So how do we reclaim this lost art? Not by scheduling stillness as another item on a to-do list. That only reinforces the productivity mindset. Instead, it begins with micro-choices. Letting a moment linger. Not picking up the phone in the lift. Sitting on a bench without headphones. Looking out the window without turning the moment into content. These small acts are not trivial—they are acts of resistance. Against acceleration. Against commodified attention. Against the lie that we are only as valuable as what we produce.

There will be friction. The mind will protest. But over time, a new baseline is established. Stillness no longer feels threatening. It feels nourishing. The inner landscape becomes less foreign. And what emerges is not a void but a fullness—the kind that doesn't need to be broadcast or shared, but simply lived.

There is a deeper philosophical question at stake here: *What kind of life do we create when we lose the ability to be with ourselves?* A life of constant distraction is a life lived on the surface. It is rich in content but poor in coherence. Doing nothing is not about escaping reality—it is about encountering it more fully. Not as curated image or efficient output, but as lived experience—messy, nuanced, slow.

This chapter will not tell you to meditate or take digital sabbaths—though those may help. It will invite you to reconsider the value of doing less, not as a strategy for success but as a stance towards existence. Because in a world obsessed with doing, *being* is a revolutionary act. And doing nothing, when approached with attention, becomes something else entirely: a doorway into depth, clarity, and connection.

What we fear in boredom is often what we most need to face. And what we find on the other side is not blankness, but the richness of a mind unburdened—a mind finally free to think, to feel, and to simply *be*.

Attention as a Spiritual Resource

What we attend to shapes us. This is not a metaphor—it is a neurological, psychological, and philosophical fact. Attention is not just a cognitive tool or a productivity asset. It is the currency of consciousness. It is the means by which the self engages the world and, in doing so, constructs its identity. And yet, in a culture where attention is perpetually mined, fragmented, and redirected by design, we have lost sight of its deeper significance. We have come to treat attention as passive, as something done *to* us by algorithms and apps. But attention is not passive. It is *creative.* It is how we build our interior worlds—and in many ways, our souls.

The phrase "you become what you give your attention to" is often repeated, but rarely examined for its depth. What does it mean to say that attention is spiritual? It begins with the understanding that attention is a form of presence. When we give something our full, undivided attention—whether it's a person, a breath, a question, or a moment—we imbue it with meaning. We do not merely *observe* it; we enter into relationship with it. And that relationship has the power to transform not just the object of attention, but the subject who attends. *To attend is to participate in the becoming of both the world and the self.*

This is not a new idea. Across contemplative traditions—from Buddhist mindfulness to Christian prayer, from Sufi zikr to yogic drishti—attention is treated as the gateway to insight and transcendence. In each of these systems, the capacity to focus, sustain, and deepen attention is considered not just a mental skill but a sacred discipline. The purpose is not merely to sharpen the mind, but to quiet it—so that something more essential can emerge: presence, clarity, compassion, insight. These are not accidental byproducts of attention. They are its natural fruits, when cultivated with care.

Contrast this with the modern attention economy, where attention is treated as a resource to be harvested, manipulated, and monetised. Social platforms, news cycles, targeted ads—all function by hijacking the attentional system, not to nourish it, but to extract value from it. The result is a collective depletion. Not only do we find it harder to focus; we find it harder to care. Attention, once eroded, takes with it our capacity for depth, empathy, and discernment. And when these faculties decline, so too does the quality of our moral and relational life.

The ethical dimension of attention is too often ignored. But attention is not neutral. What we pay attention to *we legitimise*. What we ignore, *we abandon*. In this way, attention is an act of responsibility. To attend to someone is to say: *you matter*. To attend to an issue, a wound, a moment of joy—is to bring it into the field of moral awareness. This is why distraction is not just inconvenient. It is ethically consequential. When we are too distracted to notice suffering—our own or others'—we lose the capacity to respond with integrity.

There is also a cognitive cost. Neuroscience tells us that attention is a limited resource, governed largely by the prefrontal cortex and vulnerable to depletion. When attention is split, toggled, or constantly redirected, its quality diminishes. This is not merely about productivity; it is about perception itself. The quality of our attention determines the quality of our thinking. A scattered mind cannot think clearly, feel deeply, or act wisely. And so, the degradation of attention is not just a personal inconvenience—it is a collective crisis.

To reclaim attention as a spiritual resource, we must first stop treating it as a default setting. It is not. It is a practice. One that requires intention, discipline, and—perhaps most importantly—*reverence*. Because attention is not just what we use to get things done. It is how we witness beauty, how we encounter truth, how we hold space for pain, how we experience love. These are not incidental experiences. They are the substance of a meaningful life. And they all begin with attention.

But to attend well, we must attend differently. This means resisting the cultural tendency to conflate attention with information intake. Scrolling is not attending. Consuming is not connecting. We must cultivate what psychologist and philosopher Iain McGilchrist calls "right hemisphere attention"—a form of awareness that is open, relational, and receptive, rather than controlling and grasping. This kind of attention does not dissect; it *dwells*. It allows what is present to reveal itself, rather than imposing interpretation or expectation. And in doing so, it gives rise to wonder, humility, and care.

Practically speaking, this might mean choosing to be fully present with a single task, rather than half-present with five. It might mean listening to someone without planning your reply. It might mean watching the sky change colour without documenting it. These acts are simple, but they are not small. They are the building blocks of attunement—to self, to others, to the world. And in a time of constant distraction, they are also acts of quiet resistance.

Of course, attention is not always easy. It is often shaped by forces beyond our control: trauma, stress, environmental overload. For many, the struggle to sustain attention is not a character flaw but a reflection of a nervous system in overdrive. This is why attention practices must be coupled with compassion. We do not demand stillness from a storm. We create conditions in which the wind can settle. Breathwork, nature, sleep, stillness—all help restore the physiological foundations of sustained attention. Not because they are trendy, but because they are necessary.

There is also a tension worth acknowledging: in a world that urgently needs our attention—for justice, for healing, for truth—it is easy to feel overwhelmed. The temptation is either to shut down or to attend indiscriminately, spreading ourselves too thin. But true attention is not about omniscience. It is about discernment. To ask: *What is mine to attend to, and what is not?* This question is not selfish. It is a way of preserving the integrity of our gaze—so that when we *do* give attention, it is full-bodied, wholehearted, and sustainable.

Attention, then, is not a luxury. It is a moral and spiritual imperative. It is how we meet the world—not just intellectually, but existentially. And the quality of that meeting determines the quality of our life. We do not need more content, more noise, more stimulation. We need *finer attention.* Slower attention. Sacred attention. The kind that makes room for nuance, for ambiguity, for the otherness of things. The kind that does not grasp, but honours.

To give something your attention is to give it your presence. And presence is not just what you bring into a room—it is what you *are* in that room. It is the shape of your being, expressed in where your mind rests, where your heart leans, where your eyes land. And so, to ask where your attention is going is to ask who you are becoming. Not in theory, but in practice. *Because what you give your attention to, you do not just observe—you internalise. You live with it. You become it.*

Attention is the most subtle form of intimacy. And in the end, perhaps the deepest question is not what we attend to, but how. With curiosity or critique? With openness or agenda? With reverence or indifference? These choices, made daily and often unconsciously, shape our inner lives more than any external event. They shape our values, our relationships, our understanding of self and world.

We are not just losing attention. We are losing the spiritual capacity that comes with it: the ability to be *with*—with ourselves, with others, with life as it actually is. To reclaim attention is, in many ways, to reclaim being. And that is not merely a psychological achievement. It is a sacred one.

The Dopamine Economy of Modern Life

Open a phone. Refresh a screen. Watch the likes accumulate. Check your inbox. Skip the ad. Tap. Scroll. Repeat. Beneath the surface of these seemingly trivial actions lies a powerful biochemical engine—dopamine, the molecule of anticipation and pursuit. It is the force behind the craving for one more hit of novelty, one more notification, one more rapid reward. And in the modern attention economy, dopamine is no longer merely a neurological signal. It is a *currency*—mined by tech companies, hijacked by algorithms, and traded for engagement, clicks, and behavioural data. What we are living through is not just a shift in technology or culture—it is a neurological conditioning regime at planetary scale.

Dopamine is often misunderstood. While it's colloquially referred to as the "pleasure chemical," its real function is not to produce pleasure itself but to drive *motivation and desire.* It's the neurotransmitter that underpins our goal-directed behaviour—what gets us out of bed, chasing outcomes, striving for reward. Crucially, dopamine does not spike when we receive a reward. It spikes in *anticipation* of it. This is what makes it so addictive. It's the promise of something—a hit, a ping, a win—that keeps us coming back, even when the actual experience is mediocre or fleeting.

This insight was not lost on the architects of digital platforms. Silicon Valley's most profitable inventions—endless scroll, autoplay, push notifications—are not designed merely for utility. They are engineered to create *dopamine loops*. These are systems that reward anticipation, keep users guessing, and deliver just enough unpredictability to override our natural satiety mechanisms. The result is compulsive engagement. Not because the content is always meaningful, but because the brain, hooked on the variable schedule of rewards, no longer knows how to stop seeking.

But the consequences go far deeper than distraction. When dopamine levels are consistently overstimulated—through devices, substances, or behaviours—the brain attempts to maintain balance by downregulating its sensitivity. This means that over time, the same amount of stimulation yields less satisfaction. We require more to feel the same. Novelty becomes a need, not a choice. And anything that lacks immediate payoff—reading deeply, building relationships, sitting in silence—feels intolerably slow. This is not just a psychological pattern. It is a physiological shift. The nervous system recalibrates around fast gratification, and slow satisfaction begins to feel not just unfamiliar, but inaccessible.

This is why digital detoxes often provoke unease. It's not simply that we miss the content—we miss the *stimulation.* The system, deprived of its usual dopamine spikes, enters a state of dysphoria. We call this boredom, but neurologically, it is withdrawal. And like any withdrawal, it comes with irritability, restlessness, and an almost existential sense of emptiness. But this emptiness is not a void. It is a doorway. If we can stay with it—without running back to the quick fix—the brain begins to re-regulate. Dopamine baselines normalise. We regain sensitivity to subtle rewards. Joy returns to the ordinary.

The challenge is that modern life offers few incentives for this recalibration. Our economy, our technologies, even many of our social interactions are structured around immediacy. From food delivery to dating apps to instant feedback loops, the dominant signal is clear: faster is better. But faster is also thinner. And the more we live in this high-frequency state of instant hit-seeking, the harder it becomes to dwell in depth. Attention spans shrink. Emotional resilience frays. Spiritual insight is traded for stimulation. What we lose in this exchange is not just time—it is *tonality*.

Tonality matters. Slow rewards—those that come from patience, process, and practice—nurture a different kind of being. Learning a musical instrument. Writing a thoughtful letter. Growing a garden. These acts require sustained attention, delayed gratification, and comfort with ambiguity. They do not spike dopamine; they *stabilise* it. And in that stability lies the possibility of something deeper than pleasure: fulfilment, coherence, even wisdom.

There is a growing body of research to support this. Studies in behavioural neuroscience show that long-term wellbeing is more strongly correlated with dopaminergic tone (the brain's baseline capacity to regulate motivation over time) than with frequent spikes. In other words, what matters most is not how *high* your dopamine surges, but how *stable* your system is. And that stability is cultivated not through more rewards, but through *better rhythms*—habits that align biology with integrity.

This invites a reframing. Rather than demonising dopamine—as some pop-psych narratives now do—it's more useful to see it as a *resource to be stewarded.* We need dopamine. It is what propels us toward goals, dreams, and action. But when outsourced to external systems designed to exploit its mechanics, dopamine becomes depleting rather than energising. The key is not abstinence, but discernment. Where is your dopamine going? What is it being trained to value? What feedback loops are you reinforcing with your attention?

These questions are not merely personal. They are cultural and ethical. Because when a society conditions its members to prioritise fast hits over deep engagement, it erodes the capacities most needed for a sane and humane civilisation: patience, presence, empathy, and reflection. A democracy cannot thrive on headlines alone. A relationship cannot flourish on text bubbles. A mind cannot grow on fragments. And yet, this is the architecture of much of our digital life: perpetual partial engagement, optimised for reactivity rather than reflection.

The antidote is not digital purism or asceticism. It is *a return to slower satisfactions*. These are the experiences that do not hook dopamine by spike, but by rhythm: the quiet pleasure of finishing a book, the arc of a long conversation, the satisfaction of physical work, the texture of time that is not filled, but *inhabited.* These are not nostalgic ideals—they are neurological necessities.

The philosopher Josef Pieper once warned that a society without leisure is a society without culture. Leisure, in his framing, is not idleness, but *a form of contemplative absorption in the real.* It is where we remember that not everything valuable is urgent, and not everything urgent is valuable. In this sense, resisting the dopamine economy is not a retreat—it is a reorientation. One that asks us to slow down not just in pace, but in perception. To see, feel, and know again what cannot be delivered in a notification.

This chapter will not prescribe a dopamine detox protocol. It will invite you into a different relationship with pleasure, reward, and pace. It will explore how attention, when liberated from its compulsions, becomes a site of clarity. It will challenge the myth that stimulation equals satisfaction. And it will suggest that the good life is not the one with the most hits—but the one with the most *harmony*.

Because in the end, dopamine is not the enemy. It is a mirror. It reflects what we have trained ourselves to want. And if what we want no longer aligns with what we value, the task is not to suppress the signal—it is to rewire the circuit. Gently. Daily. Intentionally. And most importantly, *slowly*.

Discomfort as a Detox Symptom

The first moments of silence after unplugging can feel surprisingly hostile. There's a distinct unease—a low-level restlessness, a mental itch, a craving for stimulation that refuses to name itself. You check your phone even though you know you've turned off notifications. You open a tab, then close it, then open it again. You sit in stillness, but the stillness doesn't feel still. It feels like something's missing. And in a sense, something is: *the constant drip of digital dopamine to which your nervous system has grown unconsciously dependent.*

This discomfort is not a sign that something has gone wrong. It is a sign that something has *begun to change*. And like all meaningful transitions, it begins not with bliss, but with friction. The early stages of digital detox can feel emotionally and physiologically dysregulating not because you're failing, but because your system is *withdrawing*. What you're experiencing is not emptiness—it's recalibration.

Most people underestimate the degree to which they are physiologically tethered to their devices. The average adult checks their phone hundreds of times per day. But it's not just the number of interactions—it's the *function* those interactions serve. They soothe anxiety, fill micro-moments, deflect boredom, interrupt emotional discomfort. Our phones have become extensions of our nervous systems. And so, when we remove them—even briefly—the nervous system doesn't know where to look. That confusion manifests as agitation, dullness, or vague unease. It's a detox symptom, and like all withdrawal responses, it reveals the depth of the dependency it disrupts.

This is a hard sell in a culture that pathologises discomfort. The implicit promise of most technologies is convenience, comfort, and control. We've been conditioned to think that friction equals failure and that any moment of unease must be resolved with a product, a solution, a scroll. But there's a deeper truth here, one that predates the smartphone by millennia: *discomfort is a necessary threshold for growth.* It is the mind's way of reconfiguring itself, the body's way of metabolising overstimulation, the soul's way of making space.

This insight is not theoretical. It is supported by neuroscience, behavioural psychology, and contemplative traditions alike. The brain, when overstimulated, downregulates its sensitivity to maintain equilibrium. The nervous system adapts to a certain frequency of input, and anything less feels like deprivation. But if you can stay with the deprivation—without immediately filling it—you begin to recover sensitivity. The brain reattunes to subtler forms of reward. The body rediscovers its baseline rhythm. The self becomes accessible again.

That said, this is not a linear process. Detox discomfort is unpredictable. For some, it appears as irritability or cognitive fog. For others, it manifests as emotional residue—old feelings that rise to the surface once the distractions are cleared. There's a reason silence retreats often provoke more internal noise than peace. When external stimulation is stripped away, the nervous system doesn't settle immediately. It often *unmasks.* It shows you what was already there, waiting for you to slow down enough to notice.

This is why discomfort is not just a symptom to be endured—it is information. It tells you what your system has been overriding. The boredom might be unprocessed grief. The restlessness might be unmet needs. The dullness might be exhaustion disguised as apathy. The key is to *stay with the signal long enough to interpret it.* Not with force, but with presence. Not with judgment, but with curiosity.

Psychologically, this is a confrontation with what Jung called the "shadow"—the parts of ourselves we exile, suppress, or ignore.

Digital life allows us to bypass this confrontation almost indefinitely. We can curate, scroll, and swipe our way past introspection. But when we unplug, even briefly, the shadow returns. And with it, an opportunity: to metabolise what we've avoided, to listen to what we've silenced, to integrate what we've fragmented.

The ethics of this process matter. Because if we frame detox discomfort as failure or weakness, we reinforce the myth that wellbeing is always pleasant. But true wellbeing—the kind that includes wholeness, not just mood—is forged through friction. It is the product of integration, not escape. And integration requires discomfort, not as punishment, but as *part of the work.*

This has practical implications for how we approach digital hygiene. If we expect detox to feel instantly peaceful or enlightening, we set ourselves up for relapse. But if we expect discomfort—if we understand it as an *essential stage*—we can meet it with structure, patience, and self-regulation. This might mean using breathwork or movement to soothe the nervous system. It might mean journalling the resistance rather than numbing it. It might mean talking with someone who understands this terrain. But above all, it means *not mistaking discomfort for dysfunction.* In fact, it is often a sign of deep function finally returning.

It is worth noting that the capacity to tolerate discomfort is a developmental milestone. In children, it correlates with emotional maturity and executive function. In adults, it correlates with psychological resilience, ethical discernment, and the ability to love without control. And yet, few of us are trained in this capacity. Most of us are trained to fix, escape, or explain. But what if we were trained to *stay*—to breathe through, to slow down, to feel without fleeing? What capacities would that unlock? What relationships would that transform?

There's an unspoken dignity in discomfort. It is the place where narratives break down and truth breaks through. It is where the performative self cracks open and the authentic self speaks. But we don't get there through optimisation. We get there through *tolerance*—of slowness, ambiguity, vulnerability. This is the magic that discomfort makes possible. Not the magic of transcendence, but the magic of recontact—reconnecting with parts of ourselves we forgot in the noise.

So the next time you unplug and feel that gnawing unease, don't reach for the nearest hit of distraction. Name it. Track it. Sit with it. Let the body register that it's safe to do nothing. Let the mind acclimate to stillness. Let the nervous system remember how to settle without stimulation. This is not indulgent. It is necessary. It is how we recover agency in an age of algorithmic compulsions.

The discomfort is not the enemy. It is the signal that the signal is clearing. And what emerges on the other side is not just calm. It is coherence. The kind of coherence that doesn't need to be broadcast or explained. The kind that simply *is*—steady, quiet, whole. And that is where the real transformation begins.

Letting the Mind Wander (Productively)

Somewhere along the way, daydreaming was demoted. It was labelled idle, wasteful, even pathological in certain educational and corporate contexts. Children were told to "pay attention" when their eyes drifted out the window. Adults, especially in productivity-driven cultures, were taught to equate wandering thought with distraction or laziness. But as neuroscience has matured, and as society begins to reckon with the psychological consequences of constant digital engagement, it's becoming clear that this dismissal was premature—and costly. Letting the mind wander is not only natural; it's cognitively necessary. And in a world saturated with external stimuli, reclaiming the cognitive freedom to meander internally may be one of the most important acts of restoration available to us.

At its core, mind-wandering refers to the brain's ability to decouple attention from the immediate sensory environment and shift it inward—toward memory, imagination, future planning, emotional processing, or abstract ideation. This is not the same as losing focus due to fatigue. It's a distinct and active mental process, associated with the brain's *default mode network* (DMN), a set of interconnected brain regions including the medial prefrontal cortex, posterior cingulate cortex, and the angular gyrus. Crucially, the DMN is most active not when we are solving a focused task, but when we are at rest—particularly during quiet, unstructured moments that allow for spontaneous mental exploration.

This insight flips much of contemporary work culture on its head. It suggests that periods of apparent non-productivity—walks without podcasts, idle gazes, moments of stillness—may in fact be the hidden engines of creativity and psychological integration. The ability to let the mind wander has been linked to improved problem-solving, enhanced creativity, deeper self-reflection, and better emotional regulation. It is, paradoxically, a highly productive state—not in the shallow sense of output per minute, but in the deeper sense of meaningful mental synthesis.

Historically, many of humanity's great thinkers have known this intuitively. Einstein famously relied on what he called "thought experiments," where he would let his mind drift and play with abstract scenarios. Virginia Woolf's fiction was steeped in the rhythms of associative, introspective thought. Nikola Tesla claimed his best ideas came to him while walking alone. These were not coincidences. They were reflections of a cognitive truth: when attention relaxes, *insight emerges*.

But the conditions required for this emergence have all but vanished from the modern cognitive environment. Digital technologies, particularly mobile ones, fill every gap. Waiting at a traffic light, standing in a queue, sitting in silence—we no longer default to internal rumination. We reach for a device. And this has consequences. Several studies, including those led by Jonathan Smallwood and Kalina Christoff, have shown that the capacity for productive mind-wandering is directly related to our ability to *tolerate boredom* and *disconnect from external stimuli.* When we lose access to these states, we don't just lose time—we lose access to a mode of thinking that is uniquely generative.

It's important here to distinguish between *ruminative* and *constructive* mind-wandering. Not all internal drift is beneficial. Repetitive, negative, self-referential thought—often a hallmark of anxiety or depression—can hijack the default mode network in unhelpful ways. The key difference lies in awareness and structure. Productive mind-wandering tends to involve the reorganisation of ideas, perspective-taking, and imaginative simulation. It can be shaped by intentional practices—like reflective walking, journaling, or gentle breathwork—that provide a container for thought without rigidly directing it.

The ethical and philosophical dimensions of this capacity are not to be overlooked. In a world where attention is increasingly commodified, the act of letting the mind wander *without external input or agenda* becomes subversive. It is a quiet declaration that not all thinking needs to be monetised, tracked, or optimised. It is a refusal to surrender the inner life to algorithms that feed on continuity of engagement. To let the mind wander is to reclaim a private space in which meaning can be made on one's own terms.

There's also a developmental angle to consider. Children engage in unstructured thought all the time—often through imaginative play or silent reflection. It's how they simulate scenarios, explore identities, and learn to self-soothe. But increasingly, this internal playground is being supplanted by screens that offer pre-fabricated stimuli. When every spare moment is filled with curated content, the child's imagination becomes reactive rather than generative. And what we do not practise, we do not develop. The risk is not just a loss of creativity, but a loss of self-directed mental autonomy.

Adults, too, are not exempt. The erosion of mental spaciousness correlates with rising levels of burnout, anxiety, and a vague but persistent sense of cognitive fatigue. Part of this is due to overstimulation, but part of it is due to under-integration. Our minds are flooded with inputs, but we are given no time or tools to metabolise them. Mind-wandering serves this integrative function. It's where dissonant thoughts find connection, where memories are consolidated, where emotion and reason get time to dialogue. It is where the scattered parts of experience are stitched back into coherence.

Reclaiming this capacity does not require dramatic lifestyle changes. It requires *micro-permissions*: the willingness to do nothing for a few minutes, to go for a walk without a podcast, to stare out of a window without guilt. It requires *designing for drift*—creating moments in your day where the mind has room to roam without redirection. This might mean rethinking your use of "dead time," reframing it not as wasted but as fertile. It might mean creating tech-free zones, not as a punishment but as a gift to cognition.

Critics may argue that in a world filled with real problems, internal drift is indulgent. But this is a false dichotomy. The capacity to attend to the world meaningfully depends on the quality of our inner attention. A distracted, fragmented mind cannot serve others well. A spacious mind can. Letting the mind wander is not escapism. It is *integration in motion.*

In truth, what we are recovering here is not a luxury—it is a birthright. To think freely, without prompt. To muse, to imagine, to mentally explore the edges of what we know and don't know. This is not dead air. It is where the mind breathes. And like all vital processes, when it is suppressed, the organism suffers. But when it is restored, something remarkable happens: creativity returns, clarity returns, *you* return.

Letting the mind wander productively is not about zoning out. It is about zoning back *in*—to a mode of thinking that precedes distraction, surpasses utility, and nourishes the whole self. It is not time off from reality. It is a deeper kind of contact with it. And in that contact lies the spaciousness we've been missing—not because we've forgotten how to find it, but because we've stopped giving ourselves permission to try.

Chapter 3
Stillness as Rebellion

Stillness is anything but passive. In an age governed by acceleration and output, choosing to pause is a conscious act—rarely encouraged and often misconstrued. It doesn't fit neatly into the prevailing metrics of success, which prize speed, productivity, and constant optimisation. To be still is to interrupt that rhythm, to step deliberately outside the slipstream of ceaseless motion. This chapter contends that stillness is not retreat, but resistance. Not resistance in the loud, performative sense, but in the quieter, deeper refusal to be reduced to urgency, deliverables, or noise.

The aversion many people feel toward stillness runs deep. Sit in a room where nothing demands your attention—no screen, no soundtrack, no schedule—and notice the itch. That subtle panic isn't nothing; it's the mind bristling at the loss of stimulation, the absence of forward motion. We often label this as boredom, but that's too simple. What we're really encountering is the withdrawal—psychic, neurological, even existential—from the drug of endless doing. Stillness doesn't strip life of meaning; it merely removes the background hum, allowing what's been overlooked to come into focus. It's not an emptiness, but a field in which coherence begins to take shape.

And yet, culturally, we treat it as suspect. Pauses make people fidget. Silence is awkward. Gaps in conversation—or in the schedule—seem to require immediate filling. There's a reason for that. We inhabit a system that thrives on extraction: of labour, attention, time. In that context, stillness feels transgressive. It halts the churn, and that—frankly—makes it dangerous. Stillness slows us down long enough to notice. To notice is to reflect. And reflection disrupts the machine.

It's time we reimagined stillness—not as idleness, but as generative space. Like fallow soil between harvests, it's where unseen processes germinate. The body, no longer braced for the next interruption, begins to recalibrate. The nervous system shifts out of vigilance.

Cortisol levels ease. The parasympathetic mode clicks in. Thoughts begin to stitch together in quieter, more patient patterns. In short, we stop reacting and start integrating. And it's in that shift, that liminal pause, that we find access to something deeper—an intelligence less mechanical, more whole.

Stillness, though, must be more than an idea. It has to land in the body. Too often, we approach calmness as another box to tick, a lifestyle upgrade, or worse, a competitive edge. But without embodiment, stillness turns brittle. It can't hold. Breathwork, grounding, and sensory awareness may seem simple, even passé, but they're not fads—they're ways of returning to the moment through the body, not the mind. Feeling one's breath as it is, or sensing the contact between foot and floor without needing to interpret, isn't escapism. It's a recalibration. It's how we remember ourselves beneath the noise.

Stillness also carries a shadow. It opens the door to all we've been avoiding: the grief, the questions, the unprocessed aches. No wonder we rush to fill the void. But emptiness isn't what meets us in stillness—it's all that's been muffled. Facing that can be uncomfortable, even disorienting. Still, the discomfort isn't punishment; it's the cost of honesty. If we want lives that are grounded rather than scattered, reflective rather than reactive, we have to let the silence speak.

This disconnection shows up in the daily grind. One task bleeds into the next. Notifications ping. Transitions vanish. On the surface, it feels efficient. Beneath, there's wear: mental fog, emotional fatigue, the low-level dread of always being behind. This isn't simply overwork—it's a kind of existential displacement. A severing from one's own rhythms. The fix isn't a weekend away or a better app. It's a new stance toward time.

That's where small rituals become powerful—not as productivity hacks, but as pattern disruptors. Making tea without multitasking. Walking without earbuds or destination. Watching clouds drift with no commentary. These moments don't move the dial on output, but they re-centre the self. They whisper, you're not a machine. And that message, repeated consistently, begins to rewire the nervous system.

From this emerges the idea of a Digital Sabbath—not as moralistic abstention, but as sacred interruption. A conscious carving out of time and space uncolonised by devices. It's not about nostalgia or tech-bashing. It's about protecting the mind's interior. A weekly act of refusal, a setting down of the scroll, a reclaiming of one's attention from the algorithms designed to fracture it. In such pauses, silence becomes a source again, not a void to fear.

Stillness as resistance doesn't require grand gestures. It doesn't insist on monasteries or hours of meditation. What it does ask is for pause—intentional, imperfect, honest. And these moments, though fleeting, accumulate. They create room for presence. They expand our tolerance for quiet. They restore a sense of scale—of what truly sustains, what actually matters.

This chapter explores that subversive pause. We'll trace the neurobiology of stillness, not to reduce it to science, but to ground its reality. We'll examine why silence unnerves us, not to scold, but to understand. We'll turn to the body—not for mastery, but for anchoring. We'll introduce daily rituals that create space—not to escape, but to re-enter life on more humane terms. And we'll explore the Digital Sabbath as a secular rite of passage—a weekly act of remembering we are not just users, but beings.

To be still in this era is to dissent. To say: I am not defined by output. I am not a node in a network. I am not available at all times. It's a refusal not just of pace, but of premise. Stillness doesn't mean turning away from the world. It means returning to it—attuned, undivided, and rooted. And in a culture addicted to urgency, that might be the most profound rebellion we can offer.

The Power of Deliberate Pause

Pause is an act of precision. In the middle of constant input, movement, and mental noise, choosing to stop—intentionally, not passively—is a radical intervention. Most people don't pause. They stop only when forced by exhaustion, illness, or breakdown. Even then, the pause is framed as a failure of momentum rather than a meaningful moment in its own right. But what if the pause is not an interruption to life, but a vital part of it? What if stillness is not the absence of action, but a *different kind of action*—one that roots, integrates, and renews?

To understand this, we need to separate stillness from stagnation. The cultural narrative that equates movement with progress and stillness with irrelevance is both pervasive and misleading. Stillness is not passive. It is generative. It is the space where thoughts ripen, emotions settle, and the nervous system downshifts from vigilance to receptivity. A deliberate pause is not a void; it is a container. And what it contains, when respected, is everything we say we long for—clarity, alignment, insight, and rest.

This isn't new wisdom. It is ancient. Across contemplative traditions—whether Zen, Sufi, Benedictine, or Taoist—pause is a practice of return. Not return to content or narrative, but to awareness itself. In these traditions, the pause is where depth becomes possible. It is where the ego's momentum falters just long enough for presence to reassert itself. And presence, unlike productivity, does not seek to prove anything. It seeks only to *be with what is*. This shift from doing to being is not escapist. It is *recalibrating*. It is how we restore coherence in a world of fragmentation.

Contemporary neuroscience supports this claim. The brain's default mode network (DMN)—active when we are not focused on external tasks—plays a crucial role in memory consolidation, self-reflection, and emotional integration. When we pause, the DMN has space to operate. Our thoughts connect across time. Our emotional experiences are processed. Our mental models update. This is not inefficient. It is essential. It is why breakthroughs often arrive in the shower, during walks, or while staring into space. These are not moments of wasted time. They are the fertile ground of synthesis.

But deliberate pause is not limited to the cognitive realm. It is physiological. When we pause consciously—especially with the body's participation—our autonomic nervous system recalibrates. The parasympathetic branch, associated with rest and repair, becomes active. Heart rate variability increases. Breath deepens. Cortisol levels drop. In other words, the body receives a signal that it is safe to stand down. Without this signal, the body remains in a low-grade defensive posture, even during so-called rest. We carry tension into sleep, digestion, conversation, and thought. A true pause resets this baseline—not as a luxury, but as a prerequisite for wellbeing.

And yet, we resist it. We fear the quiet. We fill the gap. Because to pause is to feel. To notice. To confront. And what surfaces when we stop often includes the very things we've avoided in our busyness—uncertainty, grief, fatigue, existential discomfort. The pause does not create these experiences; it reveals them. But it also *integrates* them. The deliberate pause is not for catharsis. It is for coherence. It allows the full texture of experience—pleasant and not—to be metabolised rather than suppressed.

This is why the pause must be *deliberate.* A pause that is accidental or imposed may still offer rest, but it rarely delivers integration. Deliberateness is what signals the nervous system, the psyche, and the deeper self that we are willing to *be here now.* Not just to wait for the next thing, but to *inhabit this thing.* Whether that thing is a breath, a sip of tea, a sentence not immediately responded to, or a minute of silence before entering a meeting, it is the intentionality that transforms pause from inaction into presence.

There is an ethical dimension to this as well. In systems that reward urgency and performance, pausing becomes countercultural. It is a refusal to collapse the self into output. It is a decision to value process over pace, depth over display. And that decision ripples outward. When leaders pause, cultures shift. When teachers pause, students breathe. When parents pause, children feel seen. The pause is not private. It is relational. It is how we hold space—first for ourselves, then for others.

It also reclaims *time* in a profound way. When we are constantly reacting, time feels scarce, slippery, out of reach. But when we pause deliberately, even for seconds, time stretches. We begin to experience it not as a conveyor belt, but as a spacious unfolding. This is not just poetic—it is measurable. People who engage in mindfulness practices often report a shift in time perception. Their days feel fuller, not because they are doing more, but because they are more *present* in what they are doing. The deliberate pause reorients us from chronos (clock time) to kairos (qualitative time). It reminds us that not all minutes are created equal.

Practically, cultivating the pause means building in micro-rituals that punctuate the blur of the day. Not all pauses need to be long. A breath before speaking. A still moment before sending. A walk between meetings. A window with no screen. These moments, when taken deliberately, interrupt the trance of momentum. They return us to ourselves. And the more we practice them, the more accessible they become—not as techniques, but as a rhythm of life.

But this rhythm must be protected. The world will not grant you pauses. It will ask for continuity—of thought, of content, of attention. You must *choose* to pause. You must create conditions for it. This might mean turning off notifications. It might mean reclaiming mornings or evenings as sacred space. It might mean scheduling unstructured time with the same seriousness you schedule tasks. The point is not the duration. It is the intention. Pause because it matters—not as a break from life, but as an act *within* it.

There is no blueprint for how long or how often one should pause. But what is universal is the need for it. Especially now, in a cultural climate where overstimulation has become ambient, and burnout is treated as a normal cost of ambition. We don't need more time. We need more *presence within time*. And that presence begins in the pause.

The deliberate pause is not a retreat from responsibility. It is a return to *response-ability*—the capacity to act from centre rather than from compulsion. It is how we make decisions with clarity, meet conflict with composure, and relate with genuine availability. It is how we reclaim a depth of contact—with ourselves, with others, with the moment—that is otherwise eroded by speed.

Stillness, then, is not absence. It is a presence so full, so saturated with attention, that it reveals what constant movement cannot. The deliberate pause is the doorway to this presence. Not to stop life, but to fully enter it. Not to escape, but to *arrive.* And in that arrival, we find not emptiness, but everything that makes life worth living—felt, known, and finally uninterrupted.

Embodying the Present Moment

Presence is often treated as an abstract quality—something mental, meditative, or aspirational. We hear it in workplace coaching, spiritual teaching, and wellness circles: "Be here now." Yet for many, presence remains a concept rather than an experience. The mind might nod in agreement, but the body lags behind, tense and distracted. This disconnect is not accidental. It reflects a culture that privileges cognition over sensation, performance over embodiment, and speed over somatic awareness. To reclaim presence, then, we must return not just to the moment—but to the *body*. Because *the body is the moment made tangible.* And it is through the body, not around it, that we re-enter now.

This is not a metaphor. It is a neurological fact. The brain's ability to register the present is inextricably linked to its interoceptive and proprioceptive networks—systems that monitor the internal state of the body and its position in space. When these systems are offline or overwhelmed, awareness becomes disembodied. We live in anticipation, rumination, abstraction. But when we drop into the felt sense of breath, muscle, gravity, or texture, the mind begins to stabilise. Attention stops reaching outward and starts to settle inward. *Presence is not willed—it is located.*

The challenge is that most people spend their days in a state of partial dissociation. Not pathological, but habitual. Shoulders are tense, breath is shallow, jaw is clenched—yet these signals go unnoticed because attention is elsewhere: in a screen, a storyline, a schedule. Over time, this disconnection becomes normalised. We navigate the world from the neck up, treating the body like a transport device for the brain. But the cost is profound. Without embodied presence, emotion goes unprocessed, intuition goes unheard, and stress accumulates unnoticed. The body knows long before the mind admits.

Reversing this pattern does not require radical lifestyle changes. It begins with *micro-anchors*—simple, repeatable practices that root awareness in the somatic now. Among the most accessible is the breath. Not manipulated, but *noticed.* Where is it? High in the chest? Deep in the belly? Is it tight, fast, barely there? This observational awareness—known in contemplative psychology as *bare attention*—is not about control. It is about contact. Simply noticing the breath, without trying to change it, brings the prefrontal cortex online and activates the parasympathetic nervous system. It signals to the body that it is safe to land.

Grounding is another core pathway to embodiment. While often used in trauma therapy, grounding practices are equally relevant for navigating the overstimulation of modern life. They tether the mind to sensory input—through the weight of the feet on the floor, the texture of fabric on skin, the temperature of the air, or the contact of the body with a chair. These sensations are not distractions. They are *portals.* They cut through narrative and bring the brain back to what is *real and immediate.* This shift is not just psychological—it is neurobiological. Sensory grounding activates the insular cortex, a region associated with body awareness and emotional regulation. In doing so, it gives the mind a scaffold for presence.

Movement, too, can be a profound anchor. Not performative exercise, but *attuned movement*—walking slowly enough to feel heel-to-toe contact, stretching with attention to fascia rather than form, swaying, rocking, or even standing still with awareness of micro-movements in posture. These practices remind us that presence is not a static state—it is a living rhythm. The body is always moving, even when at rest. Breath cycles. Blood flows. Muscles release. Tuning into these rhythms is a form of re-entrainment, bringing the scattered attention back into coherence with the body's tempo.

Of course, this kind of presence is not always comfortable. When we re-enter the body, we may encounter stored tension, emotional residue, or long-ignored fatigue. This is part of the work. The body is not just a tool for presence—it is also a repository of unprocessed experience. But avoidance does not resolve. It defers. And the more we defer, the more the nervous system remains in a state of subtle vigilance—always braced, always split. Embodiment is how we resolve that split. It is how we teach the body that it is no longer at war with now.

It is important to name, too, the cultural resistance to embodiment. Many societies, particularly those shaped by Western industrial and religious frameworks, have historically viewed the body with suspicion—associating it with temptation, weakness, or distraction from higher pursuits. Even in contemporary wellness spaces, the body is often instrumentalised: sculpted, optimised, or transcended. But the invitation here is not to improve the body—it is to *inhabit* it. To experience it as home, not as a project.

This shift has ethical implications. When we are disembodied, we are more susceptible to manipulation. Advertising, social media, politics—these systems thrive on disembodied attention, because disembodied people are easier to control. Embodiment, then, becomes a kind of sovereignty. It restores our capacity to sense what is true, what is aligned, what is safe or unsafe—not based on headlines or algorithms, but on the intelligence of the nervous system. The body becomes a tuning fork for discernment.

There is also a relational dimension. When we are present in our bodies, others *feel* it. We make eye contact differently. We listen with fewer interjections. We become more attuned to nonverbal cues. This creates a feedback loop of safety and authenticity. It's why embodied presence is often described as "grounded" or "magnetic." It's not charisma. It's *availability*. The body is no longer buffering experience. It is participating in it. And that participation is what allows genuine connection to take root.

These principles are not meant to become dogma or perfectionist standards. Embodiment is not a constant state. It is a practice—a returning. And that return happens in small, concrete moments: a breath before replying, a scan of physical sensation during conflict, a silent pause in a crowded room to feel the feet on the floor. These moments, though brief, accumulate. They shift the baseline. They teach the nervous system that it is possible to live *with* the body, not just in proximity to it.

Embodying the present moment, then, is not a spiritual luxury or therapeutic trend. It is a necessity. In a world of increasing dislocation—from land, from time, from each other—embodiment is what brings us back. Not to ideology, but to *sensation*. Not to distraction, but to *depth*. The practices that support this are simple but subversive. Because they bypass the intellect and speak directly to the part of us that knows—without needing to explain—when we are finally *here*.

Noise vs. Silence: A Philosophical Tension

Modern life is marked by an often-overlooked paradox: we are inundated with sound and yet deeply uncomfortable with silence. Music bleeds into elevators, cafés, waiting rooms. Podcasts accompany every walk. Notifications punctuate even our most private spaces. Noise has become a kind of default setting—ambient, expected, even necessary. Silence, by contrast, is framed as awkward or unsettling, something to be corrected with background sound or filled with commentary. This preference is not merely aesthetic. It reflects a deeper cultural and psychological tension: *we are more afraid of silence than we are aware of being shaped by noise.*

To explore this, we must begin by understanding noise not as an acoustic phenomenon but as a broader cultural force. Noise is any stimulus that demands attention without offering depth. It fills space with sensation but requires little engagement. It distracts rather than confronts. And in many contemporary settings, it functions as a kind of anaesthetic—numbing us to the discomfort of unmediated experience. Whether it comes in the form of 24-hour news, endless scrolls, chatter, or even curated "content," noise keeps us externally focused and internally fragmented.

Silence, in contrast, removes the buffer. It strips away the scaffolding of stimulation and exposes us to the rawness of presence. It is not always peaceful; it can be intensely revealing. In silence, we hear what noise allows us to ignore: the churn of our thoughts, the ache of unprocessed emotion, the question we keep postponing. Silence brings us face to face with the self. And for many, that encounter is uncomfortable—not because there is something inherently wrong, but because it is unfamiliar. *We fear silence not for what it lacks, but for what it reveals.*

This fear is not new. Philosophers and theologians have long wrestled with the tension between silence and meaning. Blaise Pascal famously remarked that "all of humanity's problems stem from man's inability to sit quietly in a room alone." For Pascal, silence was not empty—it was where existential truth emerged, unscreened by distraction. The Stoics, too, valued stillness as the precondition for reason. Eastern traditions, particularly in Zen and Taoism, treat silence not as absence but as the ground of insight. Across traditions, the message converges: *silence is not what comes after the important things—it is where the important things begin to take shape.*

And yet, our current socio-technological environment trains us in the opposite direction. From an early age, we are conditioned to equate silence with awkwardness, passivity, or deficiency. In classrooms, silence is treated as either disciplinary or disengaged. In meetings, it is often interpreted as confusion or dissent. In relationships, it is pathologised as withdrawal. But rarely is silence framed as a legitimate form of presence, contemplation, or strength. This cultural bias has implications—not just for how we interact with each other, but for how we understand ourselves.

Psychologically, the avoidance of silence often correlates with what is referred to as *low distress tolerance.* When internal discomfort arises—anxious thoughts, vague sadness, uncertainty—many instinctively reach for noise to override it. But this strategy, while immediately soothing, leads to long-term dysregulation. The nervous system never learns to settle without stimulus. Emotional complexity remains unprocessed. And over time, a kind of spiritual malnourishment sets in—the absence of real inner contact masked by the presence of constant outer input.

By contrast, those who cultivate a relationship with silence often report not emptiness, but depth. Silence allows mental sediment to settle. It creates a kind of cognitive and emotional spaciousness where patterns become visible, insight surfaces, and reactivity diminishes. This is not mystical—it is neurological. The brain's default mode network, associated with introspection, memory consolidation, and identity formation, becomes active during periods of silence and stillness. In other words, silence doesn't suppress thought—it *deepens* it.

But this deepening is not always pleasant. There is a reason so many people feel agitated during meditation retreats or silent walks. When external inputs are reduced, unresolved content rises. Grief, longing, guilt, even boredom—all of which are easier to suppress with noise—become audible. But this is precisely why silence is potent. It creates the conditions for *integration*, not avoidance. And integration is the basis of psychological maturity.

There is a moral dimension to this as well. When we live without silence, we become vulnerable to manipulation. Constant noise erodes critical distance. It disables reflection. It leaves us reactive, tribal, and cognitively fragmented. In a media landscape designed to provoke rather than inform, this is dangerous. Silence becomes a political act—a refusal to be constantly stimulated, provoked, or polarised. It is what allows us to pause before we respond, to think before we align, to remember what matters beyond the volume of opinion.

This is not to romanticise silence or denigrate sound. There are kinds of noise that are life-giving—laughter, music, conversation, protest. The issue is not volume; it is *intentionality*. Noise becomes corrosive when it is constant and compulsive—when it precludes reflection, when it replaces connection, when it is no longer chosen but automatic. Silence, similarly, is not inherently virtuous. It can be misused to suppress dialogue, enforce power, or mask complicity. The task is not to choose one over the other, but to *discern their function.*

One way to begin this discernment is to notice our immediate reactions to silence. What happens in the first ten seconds of quiet before a meeting starts? What does it feel like to walk without headphones, to sit with a partner without speaking, to let a conversation breathe without filling the gaps? These micro-moments reveal our conditioning. And they offer an entry point for change. Because silence, when practiced with intention, becomes more than a respite. It becomes a resource.

Practical integration does not require seclusion or monasticism. It begins with *deliberate absence*—moments where we choose not to fill space. No soundtrack while cooking. No default response to reach for the phone in a queue. A minute of quiet before entering a room. These pauses are small, but they are not insignificant. They train the nervous system to tolerate—and eventually appreciate—the unmediated texture of presence.

We might also begin to ask more subtle questions: Where am I using noise to avoid something? What am I unwilling to hear when things go quiet? What might silence be trying to say, if I let it speak? These are not rhetorical. They are doorways. Because the truth is, silence never lacks content. It lacks interruption. And when we stop interrupting, we discover that beneath the noise is not nothing—but *a more honest something.*

The tension between noise and silence is not merely about preference. It is about how we orient ourselves to being. Noise is often a defence against interiority. Silence is an invitation into it. And if we are to live lives of coherence—not just reaction—we must learn to move toward that invitation, even when it feels unfamiliar. Not because silence is always pleasant, but because it is *always honest.* And honesty, unlike noise, does not require amplification to be heard. It only requires that we listen.

Rituals of Slowness

Speed has become the silent default of modern life. Our attention is channelled into efficiencies, our conversations truncated, our meals consumed while multitasking. Even leisure is pressured to perform: to refresh us quickly, to fit within schedules, to justify its own worth. In such a climate, slowness is often misread as laziness, indulgence, or resistance to progress. But to move slowly—intentionally, reverently—is not to fall behind. It is to *arrive.* And arrival, in the deepest sense, is what most people are missing. We are everywhere but here. Rituals of slowness offer a way back.

The word "ritual" tends to conjure images of religion, ceremony, or tradition. But in this context, a ritual is simply a repeated act done with care and attention, imbued with meaning through intention rather than urgency. Slowness, when ritualised, becomes more than a deceleration—it becomes *a recalibration of awareness.* These practices don't ask us to escape life. They teach us how to re-enter it fully.

Consider, for example, tea meditation. In its traditional form, this practice is not about the tea itself—it is about presence. Water is boiled. Leaves are steeped. The cup is held, not hurried. Every step is an opportunity to observe: the rising steam, the changing colour, the warmth in the palm. What distinguishes this from routine is attention. The ritual creates a space in which nothing needs to be accomplished, yet everything is noticed. It's not performative mindfulness. It is *embodied stillness*. And in that stillness, the nervous system begins to slow its pace. The mind, no longer tasked with outcome or optimisation, settles into simplicity. The moment reveals its own richness—not because anything new is happening, but because we are finally *available* to what is already there.

Mindful walking is another practice often misunderstood. In a culture that treats walking as transport or exercise, slowness can feel inefficient or even awkward. But when walking becomes intentional—when we feel each footstep, notice the weight transfer, hear the cadence of breath—it shifts from being a means of getting somewhere to being an act of arriving here. In therapeutic settings, such as trauma recovery or anxiety management, mindful walking is used to anchor attention in the body, regulate the nervous system, and create a felt sense of safety in space. But its application is not limited to therapy. Anyone can benefit from the act of walking without headphones, without agenda, without a destination dictated by the clock. The walk becomes a container for reflection, integration, or simply the welcome absence of noise.

Then there are the unscripted rituals—those that arise not from formal practice but from cultivated presence. Watching a sunset, for instance, is not inherently meditative. But done without distraction, it becomes a profound exercise in attunement. The sky changes hue. Shadows lengthen. The air cools. And the observer, if still enough, begins to notice that nothing is repeated and nothing is rushed. Nature does not hurry. Yet everything happens. In such moments, slowness is not a concept. It is a rhythm—one that the body, if allowed, will remember.

Why does this matter? Because without slowness, there is no space for integration. Experiences accumulate, but they do not metabolise. The nervous system remains activated. The mind remains fragmented. Emotion is suppressed or displaced. Over time, this leads not only to burnout but to a kind of existential malnourishment—a feeling that life is passing by while we are too busy keeping up. Rituals of slowness counter this by *making space.* Not as an aesthetic flourish, but as a psychological and physiological necessity.

There is also a moral dimension to consider. Slowness allows discernment. When we are rushing, we default to habit. We react from conditioning. We consume indiscriminately—information, media, even relationships. Slowness creates the gap in which choice becomes possible. It invites us to ask: *Is this necessary? Is this nourishing? Is this aligned with what I value?* That kind of reflection is difficult, if not impossible, in a state of constant momentum.

Importantly, slowness is not about removing all speed from life. It is about introducing *rhythm.* The problem is not acceleration itself, but the lack of balance. In music, tempo without pause is noise. In life, action without reflection is frenzy. Slowness, ritualised, brings back the counterpoint. It reintroduces *pulse*—the alternation of doing and being, output and restoration, engagement and receptivity.

But this rhythm is not given. It must be cultivated. This is why slowness needs ritual. Without structure, slowness is often edged out by default urgency. Ritual gives slowness a protected space in time. It marks it as important—not because it produces anything, but because it recalibrates everything. This might look like five minutes of stillness after lunch, a walk around the block before opening your laptop, or a technology-free dusk hour in which you light a candle and let the day land before it dissolves. These are not luxuries. They are lifelines.

Culturally, this runs counter to the productivity ethic that equates worth with output. Many feel guilty for doing something "unproductive" during the day—even if that act would restore them, clarify their thinking, or make them more humane in their relationships. But this guilt is inherited, not inherent. It reflects values that prize control over connection, haste over harmony.

Rituals of slowness challenge that value system not through argument, but through *embodiment.* They show, through experience, that there is a different way to live—and that this way is not lesser, but wiser.

There is resistance, of course. Sitting still can feel vulnerable. Walking slowly can feel exposed. Even watching a sunset without reaching for the camera can feel strange. But these discomforts are part of the unlearning. They signal how deeply we've internalised the belief that presence must always be productive, that time must always be filled, that attention must always be monetised. Rituals of slowness invite us to inhabit a different paradigm—one where being *with* the moment is enough.

They also remind us that the sacred is not always found in elevated experiences or transcendent insights. Often, it lives in the ordinary made conscious. The cup held with both hands. The step taken with full awareness. The sky watched without commentary. These rituals are not means to an end. They *are* the end. And the more we practice them, the more we remember that presence does not require transformation—it only requires attention.

To live slowly, even briefly, is to make a statement about what matters. Not just for the individual, but for the collective. In a culture obsessed with speed, slowness is a form of resistance. It says: *I will not be rushed through my life. I will not reduce my attention to utility. I will not forget that being here, fully, is already enough.*

And that is why we need rituals. Not to perfect life, but to *pause within it.* To remember what pace allows the heart to be heard. To return—not just to the body or the breath, but to a kind of knowing that noise makes difficult and slowness makes possible. Not to escape, but to arrive. And in arriving, to finally realise that we were never really absent—only distracted from the quiet grace of being where we are.

Digital Sabbath: A Weekly Reset

There is a distinct anxiety that arises when reaching for a phone and finding it powered off—not due to malfunction, but by choice. That flicker of disorientation, often masked as restlessness or boredom, reveals something critical: many of us no longer *interact* with technology. We *inhabit* it. Our devices have become not just tools but environments—backgrounds to thought, mood, and identity. And in such conditions, rest is not just difficult. It becomes almost unrecognisable. Enter the Digital Sabbath: not a rejection of technology, but a weekly reorientation—*a reset for the nervous system and a remembering of the self beneath the screen.*

The language of "Sabbath" is intentionally evocative. It reaches beyond the idea of a digital detox, which often frames tech abstention in clinical or punitive terms. A detox is something you do after excess, usually with guilt or urgency. A Sabbath, by contrast, is *ritualised, rhythmic, and reverent.* It is not about escape. It is about return. It does not arise from aversion, but from value—a chosen pause that honours the need for stillness, reflection, and reconnection. For thousands of years, the Sabbath has functioned as a cultural technology to safeguard what is most easily eroded by urgency: relationship, meaning, and attention. Adapting this practice to our digital age is not appropriation. It is evolution.

A Digital Sabbath asks a simple but radical question: *What might become visible, audible, or possible if I disengaged from screens for a set period each week?* The answer varies by person, but the underlying mechanism is consistent. When we step away from algorithmic stimuli, from the compulsion to check, scroll, and respond, we create space—not empty space, but *undirected space.* This is where the nervous system recalibrates, the psyche integrates, and the imagination reawakens. In short, this is where *life outside the feed* is given a chance to surface.

But implementing a Digital Sabbath is not simply about logging off. It is about constructing a container—a structured space in time with clear boundaries, purpose, and rhythm. Without these, disconnection becomes accidental or erratic, undermining its restorative potential. The most effective Sabbaths are those that are *consistent and anticipatory*—the nervous system begins to settle not only during the Sabbath but in its approach, knowing that respite is coming. Some choose Friday sundown to Saturday sundown, echoing the traditional Jewish Sabbath. Others prefer Sunday afternoons or a set period on weekday evenings. What matters is not when, but *that it happens at all—and that it is honoured as sacred time.*

Sacred in this context does not mean religious. It means *non-negotiable and protected.* It means treating the Sabbath not as time-off, but as time *on*—on for presence, for solitude, for intimacy, for the slow reweaving of interior life. During these periods, phones may be turned off or placed in another room. Computers may be closed. The television may remain dark. More than avoidance, the Sabbath invites *replacement.* What will fill the space once digital input ceases? Reading longform. Preparing meals without haste. Napping without guilt. Taking a walk without metrics. Sitting without soundtrack. Letting the silence extend beyond the threshold of discomfort and into revelation.

Crucially, a Digital Sabbath is not a withdrawal from relevance or responsibility. It is the conditions under which relevance can be discerned, and responsibility can be recalibrated. Constant engagement dulls discernment. When we are always online, we respond to the loudest, not the most important. We react rather than reflect. A regular Sabbath reintroduces hierarchy to attention—it allows us to ask, *what truly requires my focus, and what is merely urgent noise?* That distinction cannot be made while immersed in the feed. It can only be made in its absence.

Skeptics may argue that such practices are privileged, inaccessible to those with care responsibilities, demanding jobs, or limited resources. And there is truth here. But the Sabbath does not require luxury. It requires *intention.* Even an hour without screens, practiced with consistency and depth, can function as a Sabbath. It can punctuate the blur of the week with a moment of coherence. It can create a psychic boundary between endless demand and the sanctity of attention. And when practiced communally—among families, friends, or teams—it can transform group dynamics, replacing reactive communication with more grounded connection.

There is, of course, resistance. Many who attempt a Digital Sabbath report initial discomfort: phantom vibrations, fear of missing out, a sense of invisibility. But these responses are not failures. They are *symptoms of detoxification.* They reveal just how deeply entwined identity has become with visibility, just how much stimulation we mistake for connection. These early hours of discomfort are, paradoxically, the most fertile. They signal the nervous system adjusting, the psyche emerging. Stay with them, and something subtle but profound begins to happen: *you remember how to be without being watched.*

And this is perhaps the deepest gift of a Digital Sabbath. It allows us to disentangle from the performance of presence. Online, we are always slightly on stage—curating, broadcasting, anticipating response. Even in private consumption, algorithms nudge us toward legibility. A Sabbath disrupts that dynamic. It reintroduces the quiet joy of being *off-grid*, not as rebellion, but as *remembrance of wholeness.* It reminds us that we are not primarily content creators, email responders, or productivity units. We are sensing, breathing, thinking beings—capable of noticing, of resting, of reflecting without commentary.

To be clear, this is not a call to reject technology. It is a call to *ritualise our relationship with it.* The goal is not perfection, but rhythm. The Sabbath is not a moral achievement. It is a practice of renewal. And like all meaningful practices, it evolves. Some weeks it may feel seamless, others resistant. But with time, it becomes something the body recognises—an internal exhale, a widening of space, a recalibration of self.

Incorporating a Digital Sabbath into modern life is less about withdrawal and more about *re-entry*. Not into devices, but into reality—unmediated, uncurated, unscrolled. A child's laugh not captured. A meal not photographed. A conversation not punctuated by buzz. These moments, often dismissed as mundane, are the raw material of presence. And presence, ultimately, is what all of this protects.

A weekly reset, then, is not an escape. It is *a reckoning*. With how we live. With how we've come to relate to time. With how easily our attention is outsourced. But more importantly, it is *a return*. Not to a digital vacuum, but to the kind of spaciousness in which the soul is no longer fragmented by feeds. In which quiet is no longer awkward. In which being alive is not something we perform—but something we *feel*. Unfiltered. Undivided. And finally, whole.

Chapter 4
The Mirror Effect of Technology

We often imagine digital platforms as inert tools—neutral instruments at our disposal, waiting for direction. But increasingly, they function less like tools and more like mirrors. Not the kind that shows you your physical outline, but ones that lay bare your longings, your compulsions, your inner weather. These mirrors reflect a version of ourselves filtered through algorithms, shaped by behavioural patterns and emotional tics. What we like, linger on, post, or swipe past reveals something—often more than we intend. And perhaps more than we know.

This chapter is about seeing that reflection—really seeing it. Not with a self-punishing glare, but with a steady, curious gaze. The point is not to judge, but to understand. For we do not merely use these platforms. We participate in them, contribute to them, and are subtly, continuously shaped by them.

Let's begin with a somewhat unsettling truth: your feed isn't arbitrary. It's a portrait—crafted by data, rendered by code, and based on one simple question: what keeps you there? Algorithms, though blind to nuance, are uncannily skilled at identifying patterns. They don't predict your thoughts, but they do pick up on the digital residue of your attention. Over time, this process crystallises. Your feed becomes a psychological echo chamber. That endless cascade of travel reels or fitness tips? It's not just about holidays or health. It may be signalling restlessness. Or insecurity. Or longing. The algorithm doesn't know this, of course—it merely reflects what you repeatedly gravitate toward. And therein lies its eerie brilliance.

But this mirror doesn't only show. It shapes. A fleeting insecurity becomes a loop of self-comparison. A simple desire for connection morphs into a carefully staged performance. This is the breeding ground of validation addiction—not born of vanity, but by design. These systems offer tiny, potent hits of affirmation—likes, reactions, view counts—fleeting markers of relevance. They're thin in substance, yet potent in effect. What they reinforce is not necessarily authenticity, but visibility. And in the digital economy, visibility is easily mistaken for worth.

As we internalise these dynamics, something shifts. We start tailoring our posts to what we suspect will 'land'. The spontaneous becomes scripted. The meaningful is weighed against the measurable. A persona emerges—sharpened, filtered, manicured for performance. And while it may gather engagement, it rarely brings ease. The gap between what we display and what we truly feel stretches wider. Until, eventually, it becomes difficult to recognise ourselves in our own digital footprints.

This erosion of coherence isn't superficial. It runs deep. When the less polished parts of ourselves are hidden—or worse, rendered unacceptable—we begin to feel less real, even to ourselves. The parts that rest, weep, question, or simply don't perform become suspect. We are seen, yes—but not necessarily known. What masquerades as connection ends up deepening the sense of estrangement. And in that discomfort, we scroll some more—chasing an elusive moment of resonance or relief.

Nowhere is this more pronounced than in the shadow realm of comparison. Social media, by its very structure, nudges us into constant juxtaposition. Even when we understand that we're seeing curated snippets, our nervous systems often haven't caught up. We compare our rough drafts to someone else's final edit, our inner chaos to their curated calm. It's not rational—it's relational. Our brains are wired to assess social standing, and these virtual spaces become warped social arenas. As philosopher Byung-Chul Han observed, we become performers in a spectacle of optimisation—ever improving, ever adjusting, never quite arriving.

This psychic wear and tear is often chalked up to individual fragility—just another symptom of a lack of resilience, perhaps. But that's a misreading. These aren't simply personal failings. They're baked into the platforms themselves. The system rewards speed over reflection, volume over nuance, spectacle over substance. Vulnerability that doesn't trend disappears into the void. Subtlety is punished. Depth goes unnoticed. In such an environment, to resist the metrics—to ground one's identity in something sturdier than statistics—is not indulgent. It's quietly radical.

To reclaim a sense of inner authority requires knowing when the mirror is distorting. It means learning to distinguish expression from performance. To post not to please, but to align. To recognise when we're being baited by trends that do not speak to our values, but prey on our need to be seen. It's about stepping away—not always, not entirely, but often enough to remember who's behind the screen.

This isn't easy. It asks us to swim upstream against patterns we've rehearsed a thousand times. It may mean receiving fewer likes, fewer dopamine kicks, fewer signals of digital applause. But what it gives back is harder to quantify and infinitely more precious. A quietness. A recalibration. A reminder that joy, worth, and meaning are not earned through metrics but emerge, slowly, from presence and integrity.

This chapter will trace these contours more fully. We'll look at how our feeds reflect not just our tastes but our emotional fixations. We'll examine the neural loops that bind validation to identity. We'll confront what's lost when the unfiltered self is left backstage. We'll investigate the psychological weight of envy and outline ways to transmute it, rather than let it ferment. And we'll offer pathways to reclaim authorship over your digital identity—not to craft a better brand, but to cultivate a more honest relationship with yourself.

None of this is about purism. This isn't a call to abandon the online world, nor to demonise those who embrace it. Rather, it's an invitation to wake up a little inside the scroll. To realise when the mirror has stopped reflecting and begun distorting. Because the most honest reflections of who you are aren't found in timelines or follower counts. They are found in moments of pause. In undistracted presence. In the relationships that see more than your highlights.

Technology holds a mirror, yes. But it's not the only one. Nor is it always the clearest. This chapter invites you to look again—and perhaps to look elsewhere. To remember that beneath all the layers of curation and coding, there is a self that is not seeking to be watched, but simply to be. And that this self, once reclaimed, is worth far more than any metric can measure.

Your Feed as a Mirror of the Self

Scroll long enough through any social media feed and it becomes clear: this is no longer a passive stream of updates. It is a deeply personal mirror. One that is algorithmically calibrated to show you not only what you click on, but what *clicks something open inside you.* Your feed does not reflect reality. It reflects *your reality*—or more precisely, your preoccupations, curiosities, wounds, and desires, both named and unnamed. It is a digital Rorschach test: what you see says more about you than about the content itself.

This mirroring is subtle but pervasive. Open Instagram, TikTok, YouTube, or Twitter and you are not just seeing what the world is up to—you're seeing what your attention has trained the algorithm to think you care about. This feedback loop is not evil; it's simply efficient. But the psychological implications are profound. Because what we see repeatedly shapes what we feel repeatedly. And what we feel repeatedly shapes what we believe—about others, and about ourselves.

It begins innocently. A few clicks on fitness videos after a holiday might turn into a stream of transformation reels and meal prep content. A late-night spiral into heartbreak quotes could slowly alter your baseline assumptions about love and loss. Even a search for productivity tips can devolve into performance obsession. The algorithm amplifies not just interests, but *emotional residues.* It learns to detect unresolved loops—the curiosities we can't seem to put down, the identities we're unsure about, the voids we unconsciously try to fill. Over time, your feed becomes an externalisation of your inner world: curated, coded, and monetised.

What makes this so psychologically potent is that the mirror is *interactive.* It's not like looking at a reflection in a still pond. It's more like shouting into a canyon that shouts back in distorted harmony.

The more you click, the more your content evolves—becoming sharper, more specific, more emotionally resonant. The more time you spend, the more your attention reinforces what the algorithm shows you. It's a dynamic echo chamber, not of opinions, but of *identity signals.* What draws your attention draws more of your attention. And gradually, what you repeatedly attend to starts to feel like *who you are.*

This process can be revelatory—but it can also be manipulative. Because algorithms don't care whether your attention is drawn from empowerment or insecurity, from joy or trauma. They care only that it is sustained. This means the feed is not always a reflection of your best self. It is a reflection of your *most emotionally active* self. If you're lonely, it will show you romance, longing, or connection. If you're anxious, it will feed you control strategies, threat cues, or productivity fixes. If you're insecure, it will present you with curated perfection, subtle comparison, and self-optimisation. These are not reflections of aspiration. They are reflections of vulnerability.

To complicate matters further, we are not always aware of what our behaviour is signalling. You may believe you're interested in creativity, but your screen time says you're addicted to validation. You may think you're seeking inspiration, but your scroll pattern suggests you're spiralling into comparison. This gap between conscious intent and unconscious interaction is exactly where the mirror gains its power. *It doesn't show you who you think you are. It shows you what you habitually reinforce.* And in doing so, it has the power to shape not only your perception, but your identity.

It's important to clarify that this phenomenon is not limited to a particular app or demographic. Whether you're a teenager on TikTok or a professional scanning LinkedIn, your feed is a reflection of your current psychological inputs and outputs. Even so-called "neutral" content—news, education, entertainment—carries emotional valence. What you dwell on is not determined by logic. It is governed by *emotional relevance.* And emotional relevance is often a product of what is unresolved.

This brings us to the central ethical and existential tension: how do we interact with a mirror that shapes us as much as it reflects us? How do we look without being unknowingly led?

The first answer is *awareness.* Begin to observe your feed not as a source of truth, but as a projection. Ask: What does this content say about what I'm drawn to? What needs is it speaking to—security, affirmation, novelty, belonging? What part of me is being validated, provoked, or soothed right now? These questions shift the gaze from the screen back to the self. They transform passive consumption into reflective inquiry.

Second, we must learn to distinguish between short-term resonance and long-term value. Many things feel good in the moment but corrode our clarity over time. Quick hits of outrage, humour, or envy may temporarily scratch an itch, but they rarely leave us more grounded. Begin to notice the *aftertaste* of your scrolling habits. What content leaves you feeling centred, expanded, or nourished? What leaves you anxious, depleted, or hollow? Your nervous system knows before your mind can rationalise it.

Third, reclaim intentionality. Algorithms are not fate. They respond to behaviour. This means your feed can be reshaped, but only through consistent shifts in engagement. Follow voices that challenge and inspire rather than confirm your bias. Mute or unfollow content that subtly triggers inadequacy or reactivity. Engage with material that aligns with your values rather than your compulsions. This is not about curating a perfectly positive feed—it is about *restoring alignment between your attention and your integrity.*

Finally, understand the limits of the mirror. No feed, however well-tuned, can reflect your full humanity. It cannot hold your paradoxes, your contradictions, your quiet evolutions. It cannot tell the difference between what you want and what you've learned to crave.

It cannot witness you in silence, in slowness, in ambiguity. These dimensions of self are found not online, but offline—in conversation, in solitude, in the slow texture of daily life. The digital mirror can offer clues, but it cannot offer *truth*.

This subchapter is not a call to abandon your digital life. It is an invitation to reclaim authorship over the internal narratives that digital spaces often colonise. It is a reminder that your feed is not just a reflection of who you are—it is a powerful influence on who you are becoming. The mirror is not neutral. But it is readable. And once you learn to read it, you can begin to rewrite the patterns it reflects.

To engage with your feed as a mirror is not to retreat from technology—it is to humanise it. To bring consciousness where there was once compulsion. To see not just what is shown, but what is shaping the one who sees. And in doing so, to become not merely a consumer of content, but a conscious curator of meaning, attention, and self.

Validation Addiction

A single tap on a glowing heart. A spike in comments. A modest rush when your post is shared. These may appear as harmless micro-events in the digital landscape—ordinary, even trivial—but their impact on the brain is anything but minor. These interactions are not merely social signals. They are neurological triggers, emotional cues, and increasingly, psychological dependencies. In the architecture of digital life, *likes, comments, shares, and follows have become currency—and many of us are quietly, chronically hooked.*

Validation addiction is not a metaphor. It is a behavioural loop reinforced by the same neural mechanisms that underlie gambling, substance use, and compulsive behaviours. The intermittent and unpredictable reward structure of social media—what behavioural scientists call a *variable ratio schedule*—is particularly powerful. It mirrors the mechanics of slot machines: sometimes your content gets attention, sometimes it doesn't. That uncertainty is what keeps you checking. And when the validation does come, it releases a burst of dopamine, the brain's primary reward chemical. You feel good—but only temporarily. What follows is often a subtle dip. So you post again. And the loop continues.

Unlike traditional addictions, however, validation addiction is socially sanctioned, even encouraged. It is cloaked in the language of connection, engagement, and self-expression. Few question it, because almost everyone participates. But beneath this normalisation lies a profound neuro-emotional cost: *our sense of self-worth is being externalised, fragmented, and recalibrated in real time—based not on intrinsic values, but on social metrics.* The consequences are more than psychological. They are existential.

The first casualty is *attention.* When our behaviour is shaped by the promise of feedback, our focus is no longer directed by interest or integrity—it is hijacked by anticipation. We begin to curate not only what we post, but how we think. Will this be liked? Will this resonate? Will this offend? The inner monologue becomes a strategic filter, and authenticity is compromised before it can take form. This shift is subtle but cumulative. Over time, the line between what we truly believe and what we think will perform begins to blur.

The second casualty is *emotional coherence.* Dopamine is not a standalone experience—it interacts with cortisol, oxytocin, and serotonin to shape mood and regulation. When dopamine spikes are artificially induced by external approval, they can create emotional instability. We become sensitised to feedback, increasingly reactive, increasingly needy. And because the brain adapts to stimulation, we need more approval to get the same hit. What was once satisfying becomes insufficient. The baseline shifts, and we become emotionally undernourished even when receiving attention. This is the paradox of validation addiction: the more you receive, the more hollow it begins to feel.

Social comparison compounds the problem. When likes are not just a measure of approval, but a metric for worth, they trigger a cascade of internalised ranking. We compare our numbers to others. We compare our engagement, our followers, our visibility. And because social media platforms show us the highlights of other people's lives—edited, filtered, and optimised—the comparisons are always skewed. The result is a kind of *soul fatigue*: a low-grade, persistent sense that we are not enough, even when we are seen. Especially when we are seen.

This dynamic is particularly acute among younger users, but it affects adults with equal potency. Professionals, artists, academics, activists—all increasingly feel the pressure to cultivate digital personas that align with audience expectations. The workplace has not escaped this trend either; personal branding is now part of career development. We are told that visibility is value. That if we are not seen, we are not relevant. That being liked is equivalent to being credible. These messages erode not just personal confidence, but *epistemic authority*—our ability to trust our own knowing, independent of consensus.

Validation addiction also distorts our relationship with silence. In previous generations, solitude was a space for introspection. Now, it is a void to be filled with updates, notifications, and metrics. The moment we feel invisible, we reach for proof of worth. The mind no longer settles—it scrolls. And this has profound implications for mental health. Anxiety, depression, and attention disorders are not merely rising because of content overload. They are rising because *we are living in a state of emotional outsourcing.* Our nervous systems are in a constant loop of seeking and responding, anticipating and evaluating—rarely resting, rarely integrating.

So what can be done? The first step is *recognition*. Not all engagement is addiction. The difference lies in motive and effect. Ask yourself: Am I sharing this because it's meaningful, or because I hope it will be liked? Am I checking for feedback out of genuine curiosity or compulsive reassurance? Do I feel anxious when I don't post? Do I measure my day in comments or conversations?

The second step is *interruption.* Break the loop, even briefly. Experiment with posting without checking. Or with not posting at all for a day, a week, a weekend. Observe the cravings that arise—not to shame them, but to understand them. These cravings are not moral failures. They are cues. They reveal where the need for validation has displaced the practice of self-witnessing.

The third step is *internal anchoring.* Create private rituals of self-affirmation that are not dependent on external input. Journalling. Voice notes. Unshared writing. Conversations that happen face to face, without the pressure of performance. These are not quaint alternatives—they are *neurological counterweights.* They teach the brain that approval is not a scarce commodity, but a renewable resource sourced from within.

The final step is *cultural defiance.* Validation addiction thrives because we live in a metrics-obsessed society. It is not just social media—it is quantified everything. Productivity apps. Self-optimisation hacks. Reputation scores. The pressure to measure and display our lives is relentless. To resist this culture is not to withdraw. It is to *reclaim sovereignty over how we define and express our value.* Sometimes this means posting less. Sometimes it means saying something unpopular. Sometimes it means disappearing from the feed without explanation and reappearing in real life, where affirmation is slower but more sustainable.

This subchapter is not a warning against engagement. It is a call to wakefulness. The platforms we use are not inherently corrupt, but they are structurally incentivised to exploit our emotional vulnerabilities. To participate with integrity requires more than self-control. It requires *self-awareness, self-compassion, and the courage to value presence over performance.*

To break the addiction to validation is not to reject connection. It is to *recover the possibility of connection without dependence.* Of sharing without seeking. Of expressing without expecting. Of remembering that the deepest forms of approval are not visible. They are felt in the quiet satisfaction of showing up truthfully, regardless of who is watching.

And that, perhaps, is the most radical act in the age of constant visibility: to live a life worth living *even when it goes unliked.*

Curated Selves vs. Whole Selves

If someone studied only your online presence, who would they think you are? Chances are, it would be a stylised composite—a version of you filtered through intention, aesthetics, and strategic omission. What you choose to share and what you choose to withhold are not arbitrary. They are decisions shaped by culture, psychology, and environment. And while curation is not inherently dishonest, it becomes problematic when we forget that *what we present is not all we are.* The disconnect between the curated self and the whole self is not simply a digital phenomenon—it is a modern identity crisis with emotional, cognitive, and spiritual consequences.

The curated self thrives on selection. It chooses angles, captions, affiliations, and moments that convey competence, charm, relevance, or originality. In some cases, it aims for authenticity—highlighting not just achievements but struggles, vulnerability, and "realness." But even this "authenticity" is mediated. It is what sociologists call *strategic authenticity*: selective transparency in service of relatability, not necessarily connection. In contrast, the *whole self* includes what resists articulation or packaging—the ambivalence, the grief that hasn't found words yet, the contradictions that don't resolve neatly, the internal seasons that don't trend well. The whole self is complex, unfinished, and often unshareable. And yet, it is what makes us real.

This tension between presentation and presence is not new. Humans have always crafted social identities—adjusting behaviour according to context, code-switching between roles. But digital platforms amplify this process and incentivise its most reductive expressions. On Instagram, we become lifestyle curators. On Twitter, we become punchy commentators. On LinkedIn, perpetual professionals. The medium invites the mask, and the algorithm rewards consistency. The result is a kind of character development—each of us playing the lead role in a persona we've learned will perform. But beneath this, something frays: *our ability to be whole while being seen.*

This fraying is not just psychological—it is existential. When we invest too heavily in the curated self, we risk disowning the parts of ourselves that don't perform well. Ambivalence becomes apathy. Sadness is reframed as burnout. Doubt is camouflaged with certainty. Over time, the parts of us that go unacknowledged begin to feel illegitimate. We stop showing up in our relationships with complexity. We avoid silence because it threatens to unmask what we haven't posted. We start to believe the persona is the person, even when it no longer reflects our interior world.

The emotional consequences are subtle but pervasive. Many report a sense of alienation from their own lives—not because they are lying, but because they are living on delay. Experiences are interpreted through their potential shareability. Moments are half-lived because they are half-watched—observed not through direct sensation, but through the imagined lens of an audience. This self-surveillance fractures presence. And when presence fractures, meaning erodes.

There is also the question of social consequence. When everyone else's curated self is constantly visible, the illusion of completeness becomes contagious. You don't just compare your life to someone else's. You compare your whole, complicated, evolving self to someone else's edited reel. This comparison is not merely unfair. It is disorienting. It leads to feelings of inadequacy, not because others are necessarily better off, but because *you are measuring your insides against their outside.* The curated self does not only distort the self—it distorts community. It creates a culture in which nuance is invisible and wholeness is incompatible with visibility.

So why do we curate? Why not present ourselves more fully, more honestly? Partly because the digital environment is not built for complexity. It flattens nuance. Algorithms favour clarity and frequency, not subtlety and ambiguity. But partly, too, because we have come to equate visibility with value. To be seen is to matter. And if that is the prevailing logic, then the curated self becomes a survival strategy. We show what we believe will gain approval—not because we are vain, but because we are wired for belonging. The problem is not the instinct. The problem is that the context in which it plays out now rewards performance more than presence.

The cost is profound. When we outsource belonging to feedback metrics, we lose the quiet, slow, internal knowing of worth that does not require validation. When we prioritise consistency over truth, we become less flexible, less resilient. And when we mask too often, we forget we are wearing one. Over time, this erodes trust—not just with others, but with ourselves. We become unsure of what we actually feel, believe, or want, because we've been too busy broadcasting what we think we should.

What, then, is the alternative? Not radical transparency. Not digital withdrawal. But *discernment.* A conscious distinction between *expression* and *performance*, between *connection* and *display.* Begin by asking: What part of me is making this post? What part of me is afraid not to? What might I be avoiding by curating this version of myself? These questions are not designed to induce guilt. They are tools for re-integration. They help us reclaim authorship over our digital presence—not to reject the curated self, but to *anchor it in a more honest foundation.*

Another practical approach is to make space—offline and online—for what is not immediately shareable. This might mean cultivating private creative practices that don't require an audience. It might mean spending time in friendships where silence and contradiction are welcome. It might mean showing up imperfectly, publicly, without explanation. These small acts of unpolished presence begin to restore the link between self-expression and *self*, not just persona.

The broader cultural task is to revalue wholeness. To stop applauding only what is polished and start creating space for what is real, even when it's raw. This requires not just individual courage, but collective recalibration. It means shifting our metrics of value from reach to resonance, from visibility to integrity. And it means remembering that *the parts of ourselves that don't post well often carry the most wisdom.*

To dismantle the disconnect between curated and whole selves is not to abolish curation. It is to recognise its limits. The curated self is useful. It helps us navigate visibility, signal belonging, build bridges. But it is not sufficient. A life lived only through the curated self is not a dishonest life, but an incomplete one. The goal is not to eliminate the persona. It is to *reclaim the parts of ourselves we've learned to hide.*

In the end, the deepest form of liberation is not just to be seen—it is to be known. And to be known, we must risk wholeness: showing up in ways that are not always consistent, not always neat, but always human. Because what we long for most—beneath the filters, the edits, the approval—is not to be perfect. It is to be *real.*

Comparison as a Modern Epidemic

It begins innocently enough—five idle minutes between meetings, a scroll through a feed, a glance at someone's holiday photos, their latest career update, or the morning smoothie that looks suspiciously more vibrant than anything you've had this week. What was a casual moment of disconnection becomes something else entirely: a creeping sense of inadequacy. *Why am I not doing more? Why don't I look like that? Why haven't I achieved that milestone?* Comparison, once a natural part of social life, has become a hyperstimulated reflex—one that is doing measurable damage to our self-concept, emotional regulation, and collective wellbeing.

To understand why comparison is so corrosive in the digital age, we must first understand its evolutionary roots. Social comparison is an ancient mechanism. From an anthropological perspective, it was essential for navigating group dynamics—assessing hierarchy, identifying threats, determining alliance. Psychologist Leon Festinger formalised this with his Social Comparison Theory in the 1950s, noting that humans evaluate themselves not in isolation, but in relation to others. We seek out people similar to us to gauge how we're doing. We use others as mirrors, not only to understand our status, but to affirm our identity.

But in Festinger's time, the comparisons were limited. You could only compare yourself to your immediate social circle—colleagues, neighbours, acquaintances. Today, that circle is global, relentless, and curated to provoke. Digital platforms have radically transformed the landscape of comparison. We are now comparing ourselves *not just to peers, but to the most performative moments of everyone, everywhere, all the time.* The playing field is neither fair nor neutral. It is algorithmically optimised to provoke engagement—and nothing engages quite like envy.

Platforms like Instagram and LinkedIn are visual theatres of success, attractiveness, and social capital. They present a veneer of perfection that is both aspirational and unattainable. Photos are filtered. Achievements are polished. Failures are edited out or reframed as triumphs. This is not deception; it is *curation.* And yet, our brains are ill-equipped to process these images as partial truths. We compare our internal chaos to someone else's external coherence, forgetting that what we are seeing is a performance, not a person.

The emotional toll is cumulative. Studies across disciplines—from psychology to behavioural neuroscience—have documented the link between social media use and increased symptoms of depression, anxiety, and low self-esteem. A 2018 study published in *Journal of*

Social and Clinical Psychology found that limiting social media use to 30 minutes per day significantly reduced feelings of loneliness and depression. Another by the Royal Society for Public Health in the UK identified Instagram as the most detrimental platform for young people's mental health, largely due to issues of body image and comparison.

But the problem is not just with adolescents. Professionals in their thirties, forties, and fifties report heightened stress and burnout linked to social comparison. "LinkedIn anxiety" is a real phenomenon: the sense of inadequacy provoked by the constant stream of promotions, publications, and professional accolades. Even within wellness communities, comparison takes a toll—those with the most "mindful" lives often showcase routines that are inaccessible to most. The yoga retreat in Bali, the plant-based perfection, the seamlessly balanced work-life ethos—these images suggest not only what is desirable, but what is *expected.* And failing to meet those expectations, even implicitly, creates shame.

This shame operates on a deep level. It is not simply "I don't have what they have." It is "There must be something wrong with me for not having it." This shift from external envy to internal deficiency is what makes comparison so insidious. It triggers self-doubt not just about our circumstances, but about our *character.* And because shame thrives in silence, we rarely name it. Instead, we scroll more. We seek more. We post more, hoping—consciously or not—to tip the scales back in our favour. To become the person someone else might envy.

So how do we interrupt this cycle? The first and most critical tool is *awareness.* Begin to notice your triggers. Does certain content consistently leave you feeling less than? Pay attention to your body: tension in the jaw, a tightening in the chest, a sudden fatigue. These are physiological cues of comparison fatigue. Don't dismiss them. Track them.

The second tool is *discernment.* Recognise the difference between inspiration and inadequacy. Inspiration energises. It opens possibility. In contrast, comparison depletes. It narrows your sense of what's possible by framing success in someone else's terms. Ask yourself: *Is this content expanding me, or diminishing me?* And equally: *Is my reaction about them, or about a part of me I have yet to affirm?*

Third: *de-normalise perfection.* The curated lives you see online are not lies, but they are not whole truths either. Every beautiful photo is backed by unseen labour, every accolade by silent failures. Complexity is the rule of life, not the exception. Seek out creators who are willing to share nuance, not just narrative arcs. And more importantly, be willing to *see yourself* without a performance filter.

Fourth: *reclaim your own metrics.* The algorithm does not know your values. It rewards what is loud, not what is true. If you measure your life by likes, you'll build a life optimised for visibility, not meaning. Return to your own standards: Did I act in integrity today? Did I connect deeply? Did I create something that matters to *me*? These questions are quiet. They don't trend. But they are the foundation of a life that feels real.

Finally: *cultivate offline reality.* Comparison flourishes in abstraction. It fades in the presence of actual human interaction. Speak with people in real life, especially those who are not part of your online ecosystem. Volunteer. Teach. Listen. Serve. These acts re-centre you in communities where value is lived, not displayed.

The goal is not to eliminate comparison entirely. That is neither realistic nor necessary. The goal is to *contextualise it.* To see it as a signal, not a sentence. To use it not as a mirror, but as a compass—pointing not to where you should go, but to what you need to return to in yourself. Beneath every pang of comparison lies a deeper longing: to feel worthy, visible, and enough. The platforms cannot give you this. But they can teach you, through their distortions, where your truest values lie.

And that is the quiet liberation in all of this. Not to scroll less, but to *compare less destructively.* Not to stop watching others, but to *start witnessing yourself* with greater clarity and compassion. Not to reject ambition, beauty, or excellence—but to *redefine them on your own terms*, grounded in a selfhood that is not swayed by metrics, but anchored in meaning. Comparison may be a modern epidemic. But awareness is its antidote. And attention—conscious, deliberate, sovereign attention—is the cure.

Reclaiming Inner Authority

You are being shaped right now. Every scroll, swipe, and click subtly trains your mind in what to value, who to emulate, how to feel about yourself. This shaping is not neutral. It is engineered. And while we like to think of ourselves as sovereign agents—choosing what we consume and how we respond—the architecture of digital life is designed to bypass conscious choice. In this landscape, *reclaiming inner authority is not just a philosophical aspiration; it is a practical necessity.* Because the alternative is to live a life authored by the screen—curated by algorithms, validated by strangers, and slowly disconnected from our own inner compass.

To reclaim inner authority is to remember that *you are the narrator of your experience—not the algorithm, not your audience, not the trending topic of the week*. It is to locate the source of value, meaning, and orientation within yourself, rather than outsourcing it to likes, metrics, or cultural consensus. This is neither easy nor intuitive in an environment that constantly seduces us into external referencing. But it is vital, if we are to restore psychological clarity, emotional resilience, and spiritual alignment.

We begin with the problem: *digital environments increasingly condition our sense of self through external metrics.* The quantification of identity—followers, views, engagement rates—recasts worth as a visible, trackable phenomenon. This is not inherently dangerous until those numbers begin to replace more grounded forms of self-understanding. A piece of writing feels worthwhile only if it goes viral. A moment of beauty is validated only if it's shared and appreciated. Even acts of service or creativity are subtly reframed through their potential for exposure. We begin to experience ourselves not as living beings with intrinsic value, but as performers in a reputational economy—constantly managing impressions, optimising visibility, and measuring success in the currency of attention.

This erosion of inner authority is reinforced by the *architecture of the platforms themselves.* They reward emotional reactivity over reflection, speed over depth, popularity over nuance. In such an ecosystem, thoughtful pauses and internal inquiry are not just discouraged—they are rendered invisible. The algorithm has no metric for what is meaningful to *you*, only for what will keep you engaged. The result is a dislocation of attention from the inner world to the external signal. You begin to feel anxious when the phone is quiet. You second-guess your instincts. You seek validation before you seek clarity. You become disoriented—not because you've lost your values, but because you've stopped listening to them.

But here's the quiet, disruptive truth: *inner authority can be rebuilt.* It is not a mystical state or a fixed trait. It is a practice—of paying attention differently, of deciding what matters before the world decides for you, of letting your values shape your behaviour rather than your feed. And it begins with *attention hygiene.* Not just consuming less, but *consuming more consciously.* Notice what hijacks your mood. Track which voices leave you fragmented or diminished. Audit your digital diet with the same seriousness you'd apply to food or finances. Your attention is a finite resource. Spend it where your values live.

Next, *re-engage your own inner voice.* For many, this voice has gone quiet—not because it disappeared, but because it's been drowned out. Begin to ask yourself: *What do I actually think?* Not what's trending. Not what will be applauded. What feels true in my body? What resonates in silence? You don't need to publish the answer. You just need to trust it. Practices like journaling, unscripted speaking, or even private rituals of articulation can help reconnect the mind with its deeper knowing. And crucially, resist the urge to immediately externalise those insights. Let them live in you first. Let them root.

Another critical shift is the movement from performance to presence. Reclaiming inner authority requires *decoupling expression from validation.* You are allowed to write something that no one reads. You are allowed to make art that never sells. You are allowed to have thoughts that are not opinions. The internet has convinced us that everything must be shared, monetised, and branded. But inner authority flourishes in spaces that are *unmonitored.* Make time for work that is witnessed only by yourself. Not because it's private—but because it's *yours.*

Also, cultivate *discernment over consensus.* This does not mean becoming oppositional for its own sake. It means building the capacity to think independently—even when your thoughts go against the grain. In an age of echo chambers and virality, inner authority requires the courage to hold unpopular truths, to tolerate ambiguity, and to resist the pull of ideological conformity. Read widely. Engage deeply. Challenge your assumptions. But always return to this question: *Does this feel aligned with what I know, not just intellectually, but viscerally?*

Reclaiming inner authority also requires a deep redefinition of success. The modern digital ethos equates visibility with value. But this is a dangerous conflation. Visibility is a function of platform dynamics. Value is a function of *alignment.* The most impactful work is often not the most visible. Some of the most fulfilled people you will ever meet are not online at all. Success, when defined from within, rarely looks like dominance. It looks like *integrity, consistency, contribution, and peace.* These metrics don't show up on dashboards. But they show up in how you sleep, how you love, and how you show up to your own life.

Of course, this reclamation will not be linear. You will slip. You will seek validation again. You will get caught in metrics and applause.

That's not failure. That's feedback. Let it remind you to return—not with shame, but with curiosity. Each return strengthens the muscle. Each pause is an act of authorship. Each refusal to let an algorithm define your worth is a quiet revolution.

What's at stake here is more than mental health. It is *authentic agency*. Without inner authority, we are highly suggestible—more likely to adopt borrowed beliefs, pursue hollow goals, and perform selves we do not recognise. But with it, we regain the ability to make choices that are *ours*. Not reactive. Not performative. But grounded. Conscious. Free.

You do not need permission to reclaim your inner compass. You do not need consensus to follow it. You are allowed to choose what you value, even if it makes you invisible. You are allowed to trust your instincts, even when they are inconvenient. You are allowed to author a life that is not optimised for attention—but for coherence, depth, and truth.

And in doing so, you become something rare in the modern world: *self-sourced, self-trusting, and sovereign.* Not because you have the loudest voice—but because you know where it comes from.

Chapter 5
The Body Remembers What the Mind Scrolls Past

Despite the current cultural obsession with digital detoxes, mental clarity, and the pursuit of mindfulness, there remains one area that's conspicuously neglected in discussions about overstimulation: the body. Not the stylised, sculpted body that appears in filtered photos and curated timelines—but the one that pulses quietly beneath all that noise. The one that breathes, flinches, aches. The body that bears the weight of our experiences when the mind, distracted and overstimulated, skims over them. While our minds zip from image to headline at a frenetic pace, the body digests everything more slowly, more thoroughly. It doesn't argue. It absorbs. It doesn't rationalise. It reacts. And, after a time, it resists.

Let's begin, then, with a provocation: what if the fatigue, irritability, and ambient tension so many of us feel has less to do with what we think—and far more to do with what we feel, but have not yet named? What if the source of our modern unease lies not in our psychology, but in our physiology—in nervous systems that are no longer attuned, but overloaded? The digital age has trained our minds to be relentlessly active, while our bodies have grown quiet, almost passive. This split severs a crucial feedback loop—one meant to tether us to the present moment. And until we repair that loop, no amount of mental decluttering will bring us home to ourselves.

We're used to hearing that screens reshape the brain, and yes, they do. But the subtler, more insidious impact plays out in the body. Every ping, buzz, or flashing banner draws a reaction—micro-movements of tension that register not as thoughts, but as somatic flinches. The shoulder stiffens, the breath shallows, the posture caves inward. Even idle scrolling dampens our sensory acuity and throws off sleep cycles. These aren't side effects; they're physiological messages. And they rarely scream. Instead, they accumulate—quietly, steadily—until they're dismissed as vague tiredness, or chalked up to bad habits. But make no mistake: the body knows. It always has.

This saturation registers in the language of the flesh: tense jaws, clenched hips, erratic digestion, a nervous system caught in perpetual low-grade alert. These aren't random symptoms. They're adaptive responses. The body is not malfunctioning—it's accommodating. It adapts to the hyperstimulation of our devices by bracing, suppressing, recalibrating. It stifles hunger cues. It downplays exhaustion. It dulls its own signal. And in doing so, it forgets how to rest without distraction, how to move without instruction, how to exist without validation. This is the price of living too long in disembodied states: we lose not just vitality, but intimacy with our own interior.

But let's be clear—this isn't a dirge. It's an invitation. A call to come back to the body—not as something broken to be hacked or fixed, but as something inherently wise, waiting to be listened to. And this return doesn't demand grand gestures. It starts small. A breath released all the way to the bottom. A stretch that has no goal. Noticing the press of your feet against the ground. Feeling the coolness in the air as you step into a room. These are not distractions from the digital—these are antidotes. Tiny, bodily acts of resistance. Repatterning. Remembering.

In the pages ahead, we'll look closely at how the traces of digital life imprint themselves into our physical form—and how to read those traces. We'll explore what it means to reset the senses, to reawaken touch, scent, sound, and space as pathways home. When our attention is constantly siphoned outward, the senses become dulled. But when gently re-engaged, they can serve as anchors. This isn't just about regaining focus—it's about restoring our ability to feel fully, from the skin inward.

Next, we'll shift the lens to movement—specifically, the kind that doesn't look like much. Not workouts, but micro-movements. The tilt of a neck, a hand pressed to the chest, a soft rock side to side. These movements aren't performative. They're signals to the nervous system: you're safe now. The storm has passed. And without those messages, even the most profound mental insight can land hollow. The body must believe it is safe in order to truly settle.

We'll also explore a deeper metaphor: the body as a kind of technology. Not the mechanical, linear kind, but a sacred system—an instrument honed over millennia. Long before apps told us how to optimise sleep, the body responded to dusk and dawn. Long before heart-rate trackers, it knew when to slow, when to quicken. That intuitive calibration has been crowded out, its subtlety drowned in data. But it hasn't disappeared. It simply waits—for silence, for attention, for return.

Which brings us to the larger question: in a time when so much of life has become virtual, what does it mean to be flesh? To touch, to tremble, to move not for show, but from instinct? Disembodiment isn't just a physical drift—it's an existential one. To reclaim the body is to reclaim aliveness. Not as a lifestyle trend or aesthetic pursuit, but as a form of remembering: that we are creatures, not content. That healing doesn't always look like progress, but often like stillness, rhythm, and slowness.

This chapter doesn't offer a how-to manual. It isn't prescriptive. Instead, it sketches a map—not a perfect one, but one you can feel. It invites you to notice, to listen, to reawaken a relationship with your own physicality. Not in the name of performance, but in pursuit of truth. Because while the mind can argue its way out of disconnection, the body cannot lie. It will keep score. It will wait. And when you're ready, it will show you how to come home—not through effort, but through presence. Through breath. Through the undeniable sensation of being alive in a world that rarely asks you to feel it.

Somatic Traces of Digital Overwhelm

The body does not lie. Long before the mind can articulate that something is off, the body signals it in sensation: a jaw clenched without awareness, a breath held in the chest, a subtle tightening in the gut. These signals are often dismissed as minor irritations or idiosyncrasies. Yet they are the very markers of something deeper—*a nervous system attempting to adapt to a level of stimulation it was never designed to process*. In the age of constant connection, the real cost is not merely digital fatigue. It is physiological dysregulation. And the body, more than any device or dashboard, is where that cost is most accurately registered.

Digital overwhelm is a state of cumulative nervous system activation, triggered not by a singular traumatic event but by relentless micro-stimuli. Notifications, content overload, screen glare, algorithmic unpredictability—each of these imposes a low-grade stress response, subtly activating the sympathetic nervous system. This response is often so ambient that we hardly notice it. We do not collapse or panic. Instead, we live in a sustained *"on"* state: hypervigilant, subtly braced, constantly toggling between tabs, tasks, and timelines. Over time, this state becomes our baseline. We confuse it for normal.

Physiologically, however, the impact is significant. Take breath, for instance. The modern screen user, particularly under stress, breathes in short, shallow sips from the upper chest. This pattern—technically called thoracic breathing—triggers a feedback loop in the nervous system. Shallow breath signals to the brain that we are not safe, activating further stress hormones like cortisol and adrenaline. The result? Increased heart rate, diminished immune function, impaired digestion, and heightened emotional reactivity. All of this can happen while simply responding to emails.

Muscle tension follows a similar logic. The eyes, locked on a screen, transmit strain to the jaw, neck, and shoulders. Repetitive postures, especially when performed under stress, lead to muscular holding patterns that can persist long after the device is closed. The jaw, in particular, is a common repository for unprocessed tension. Many grind their teeth or clench unconsciously during screen-based tasks. This is not simply ergonomic—it is somatic. It is the body's way of bracing for stimuli it cannot predict or escape.

Sleep, too, suffers. Blue light exposure is only part of the problem. The larger issue is *cognitive arousal.* Screens—especially at night—fill the mind with unresolved narratives, unresolved tasks, and unresolved comparisons. Even after logging off, the nervous system remains activated. Melatonin production is suppressed. Sleep latency increases. The quality of rest declines. What masquerades as mental overstimulation is, at its core, *neurochemical interference.* The body does not drift into rest when it is unsure it is safe. And digital life, with its constant demands and open loops, rarely offers that assurance.

These effects are not reserved for tech workers or social media users. They appear in teachers scanning student portals, in parents managing digital calendars, in healthcare workers navigating EMRs. The medium varies, but the pattern is consistent: overstimulation outpaces regulation. And the body becomes the holding place for what the mind refuses to process.

What, then, can be done?

The first step is *somatic literacy*—learning to recognise the body's cues not as annoyances but as data. That afternoon headache might not be about dehydration. It could be information fatigue. The tension in your shoulders might not stem from bad posture but from the emotional labour of curating your digital presence. These sensations are not interruptions to your productivity. They are invitations to recalibrate.

Begin by tracking *where* in the body you feel digital stress. Is it the jaw? The eyes? The diaphragm? Set a timer three times a day and take thirty seconds to scan for tension—not to fix it, but to *acknowledge it.* This simple act of witnessing can begin to interrupt chronic holding patterns. From there, introduce gentle interventions. *Extend the exhale.* The exhalation is linked to the parasympathetic nervous system—the part responsible for rest and repair. A longer exhale sends a clear message to the body: there is no threat here.

Another entry point is through *movement.* Not the kind tracked by a fitness app, but the kind that emerges from sensation. Roll your wrists. Sway your torso. Walk slowly with attention to the soles of your feet. These movements may appear trivial, but they are neurologically potent. They signal to the body that it is safe to unfreeze, safe to soften. Over time, these gestures restore what digital life fractures: the sense that we inhabit a body, not just a profile.

Sound is another powerful tool. Because hearing is linked to the vagus nerve, certain tones—especially low-frequency or rhythmic ones—can help down-regulate the nervous system. Consider using chimes, ambient music, or even humming as micro-practices during the day. The goal is not relaxation per se, but *reconnection*: helping the body remember that it has rhythms beyond the buzz of a device.

Importantly, these interventions must not become another project. The modern self-help paradigm often turns embodiment into a checklist, a performance. This chapter advocates the opposite. *Let the body lead.* You do not need to track your calm. You need to *feel it.* And that feeling cannot be forced through willpower. It must be allowed through practice.

This is where we must challenge a deeper cultural bias: the notion that cognition is the highest form of intelligence. In fact, the body processes information far faster than the conscious mind. It detects dishonesty in tone before the words are understood. It flinches at digital tension before the mind can name anxiety. It knows, long before we do, when we've had enough. The tragedy is that we've been trained to override this knowing in favour of productivity, engagement, and mental clarity. But clarity, real clarity, begins in the body.

Reclaiming somatic awareness is not just about comfort—it is about *reclaiming agency*. A regulated body resists manipulation. It is harder to sell to. Harder to shame. Harder to addict. Because it has *a reference point* beyond the screen. A sense of aliveness that does not depend on performance. A sense of worth that does not require witness. This is not poetic idealism. It is physiological truth.

In this way, the body becomes not only a site of healing, but a site of resistance. In a culture that commodifies attention and exploits stress, tending to the body is a radical act. A soft jaw is subversive. A deep breath is a refusal. A rested body is a declaration: *I do not belong to your metric.*

This chapter is not about optimisation. It is about *remembrance.* Remembering that beneath the mind's pace and the screen's pulse, the body has been waiting—not for content, but for contact. And in every stretch, breath, and sigh, that contact becomes possible again. Not later. Not after the next notification. But now.

Reset Through the Senses

There is a silent irony at the core of modern overstimulation: the more information we consume, the less we actually *feel.* In an age where the mind is relentlessly occupied—chasing deadlines, scanning headlines, tracking metrics—the body is often forgotten. Or more accurately, it is overridden. The result is not just stress, but disconnection. The body loses its ability to self-regulate, not because it is broken, but because its feedback loops have been drowned out by digital noise. The remedy is not intellectual—it is *sensory.* If you want to come back to yourself, you must come back through the senses.

This is not new wisdom. It is old, elemental, and human. Every wisdom tradition, from indigenous earth-based cultures to contemplative monastic lineages, has recognised the body's sensory faculties as gateways to presence. Today, neuroscience confirms what sages long intuited: the senses are not just passive channels—they are active portals of regulation. When consciously engaged, they provide a direct pathway to parasympathetic activation, helping the nervous system transition from overstimulation to calm. This chapter is a guide to using those portals with care, intelligence, and immediacy.

Begin with *touch.* Touch is the first sense to develop in the womb and the last to fade in dying. It anchors us in reality faster than almost anything else. When the mind is spinning, reaching for your own forearm and applying gentle pressure can be more effective than a thousand mental affirmations. This is not sentimental; it's neurobiological. Skin is densely populated with receptors that send safety signals to the brain, particularly when the touch is slow, intentional, and self-generated. Weighted blankets, palm-stroking, or placing one hand over the heart and one on the belly—these are not wellness clichés; they are primitive acts of grounding. And they work, often within seconds.

For those navigating digital fatigue, *temperature contrast* can be an immediate reset. Cold water on the wrists. A warm compress over the eyes. The shift in temperature provides a jolt to the nervous system that is far gentler—and more effective—than a caffeine spike. It anchors you in the present moment by stimulating mechanoreceptors and thermoreceptors that are wired into the autonomic system. This is why practices like cold plunges or hot baths have gained traction—they tap into ancient physiological pathways that modern life has muted.

Next is *scent.* Often undervalued, the olfactory system is the only sensory modality that bypasses the thalamus and connects directly to the limbic brain—the seat of memory and emotion. This is why a single inhalation of a familiar aroma can instantly evoke safety, longing, or calm. Essential oils like lavender, bergamot, or frankincense are not merely fragrant; they are chemical messages to the nervous system. But scent need not be commodified. The smell of rain, earth, firewood, or even your own skin post-sunlight can serve the same function. To work with scent consciously is to remind the body that the world is not just visual and verbal. It is *sensory terrain.* And that terrain can stabilise us.

Sound is equally potent—especially sound with intention. The constant noise of digital environments—notifications, ambient chatter, algorithmically curated audio—keeps us in a reactive state. But sound, when used deliberately, becomes a tool for coherence. Binaural beats, singing bowls, chimes, or even slow instrumental music with minimal lyrics can entrain the brain toward alpha or theta states. These are not abstract concepts—they are measurable brainwave patterns associated with rest and integration. More accessibly, humming or chanting gently engages the vagus nerve, stimulating the relaxation response from within. Silence, too, is not an absence. It is a form of sound that restores the body's ability to hear itself.

And then, *movement.* Not exercise. Not performance. *Movement as sensing.* We live in an era where physicality is often measured—steps tracked, calories counted, forms perfected. But the body craves movement that is not tracked, not judged, and not extractive. Gentle swaying, stretching, swiping the arms through space—these actions reintegrate the sensory-motor loop, returning the body to itself. Try lying on the floor and rotating your wrists. Rock from side to side without purpose. Let your spine coil. These gestures remind your nervous system that you are not just a mind moving a body. You are an organism with internal rhythm. A being designed for wave, spiral, and breath.

When the sensory system is engaged fully and mindfully, something subtle but profound occurs: *the body comes back online.* This doesn't mean a sudden epiphany or dramatic breakthrough. It means a quiet restoration of presence. You are no longer scattered across tabs, feeds, or timelines. You are here. In sensation. In breath. In the *now.* And from that place, the mind naturally slows. The emotions begin to metabolise. Decision-making clarifies. Life stops feeling like something to manage and starts feeling like something to *inhabit.*

None of this requires hours of free time or special tools. Sensory grounding can happen in thirty seconds. You can press your feet into the floor during a Zoom call. You can close your eyes and listen to the hum of your refrigerator. You can hold a cup of tea and trace its warmth into your fingers. These are not indulgences. They are correctives. They reverse the disembodiment that modernity normalises.

The ethical implication is worth noting. A disembodied population is easier to distract, manipulate, and exhaust. A sensually attuned individual—one who *feels their own skin, hears their own breath, senses their own limit*—is far less susceptible to systemic overwhelm. The sensory body becomes a site of resistance. You are no longer just data to be harvested. You are a sovereign field of perception. And perception is power.

This chapter, then, is not just about calming down. It is about waking up—through the senses. Not abstractly, not later, not when you have more time. Now. With your skin. Your breath. Your spine. Let each be a doorway. Let each be a return. Because your body does not live in yesterday or tomorrow. It lives here. And here is where healing begins.

The Power of Micro-Movements

There is a prevailing myth in modern wellness culture that meaningful transformation requires major effort—full routines, lengthy commitments, dramatic overhauls. It's a notion reinforced by performance-driven paradigms: if it's not intense, it's not effective. But the nervous system doesn't respond to pressure in the same way the ego does. It does not heal through heroic interventions. It re-regulates through *consistency, subtlety, and safety*. And in this context, the most potent shifts often come not from grand gestures, but from *micro-movements*—small, intentional actions that realign the body and reorient the mind from the inside out.

Micro-movements are not a form of exercise, nor are they a productivity hack. They are, at their core, *a language of communication between body and brain*. Closing your eyes for ten seconds, rolling your shoulders once, pressing your feet into the ground, releasing a sigh—these acts do not *look* transformative. Yet physiologically, they disrupt patterns of tension, re-establish somatic coherence, and signal to the nervous system that it can let go of hypervigilance. What you are doing, in effect, is offering the body a brief but powerful reminder that presence is possible. And in today's hyperstimulated environment, that reminder is nothing short of radical.

To appreciate the impact of micro-movements, we must first understand the context they're responding to. Most people now live in a state of *low-grade sympathetic activation*. This is not a full-blown fight-or-flight response, but a more insidious version: chronic muscular tension, shallow breathing, and subtle postural collapse—what some somatic therapists call "digital bracing." It is the body's way of trying to remain alert in an environment that never truly quiets. Over time, this leads to what neurologists refer to as *allostatic load*: the cumulative burden of chronic stress on the system. The body adapts to constant activation not by finding balance, but by normalising imbalance.

Micro-movements intervene in this process by shifting the autonomic nervous system away from sympathetic dominance toward *parasympathetic accessibility*—that is, into a state where rest, digestion, and repair can resume. The science behind this is both elegant and accessible. When you elongate your exhalation, for example, you stimulate the vagus nerve, which plays a key role in regulating the parasympathetic branch. A single long exhale, especially if accompanied by a softening of the eyes or jaw, can begin to down-regulate the system. This is not anecdotal. It is physiological fact.

The same is true for stretching—not as fitness, but as feedback. When we stretch slowly and without force, especially during moments of stress or digital saturation, we introduce novel input to the sensory-motor cortex. The brain receives this input not just as movement, but as *information*: the threat is not immediate, the environment is not hostile, the body is still under conscious control. This is why even brief movements—lifting the arms overhead, twisting gently at the waist, tapping the fingers rhythmically—can interrupt cycles of mental rumination and bring attention back to the body. The shift is not just psychological. It is *neurochemical*.

What makes micro-movements uniquely valuable is that they are *accessible*. They require no equipment, no time block, no specialised training. They can be performed during meetings, on public transport, between tasks. They are portable interventions, always available to those who know how to use them. And crucially, they are non-performative. Unlike most modern fitness modalities, which often replicate the pressures of productivity culture, micro-movements are not measured by intensity or outcome. Their value lies in their *intimacy*: how directly and gently they communicate with the nervous system.

Consider, for instance, the simple act of placing your hand on your chest and applying slight pressure during a stressful moment. This is not self-soothing in a metaphorical sense. It is literal, tactile input that engages mechanoreceptors in the skin and fascia, which in turn send signals to the brain that disrupt the threat response. Or think of the act of slowly circling the neck—not with force, but with awareness. You are not only releasing muscular tension; you are *reclaiming proprioception*—your internal map of where your body is in space. And that awareness, once restored, reintroduces agency.

There is also a deeper philosophical argument for micro-movements: they help undo the binary between movement and stillness. We tend to think of ourselves as either active or inactive, doing or resting. But the body is never truly still. It pulses, breathes, shifts subtly. Micro-movements align us with this truth. They teach us that regulation is not something we *do*—it is something we *allow*. By honouring the body's natural rhythms and responding to its signals in real time, we foster a sense of internal continuity that modern life constantly disrupts.

This has emotional implications as well. Micro-movements create space for *emotional digestion*. Emotions are not cognitive events. They are physiological episodes that require movement to metabolise. Anger rises in the jaw and fists. Grief contracts the chest. Anxiety hums in the diaphragm. When we move, even slightly, we invite these emotions to complete their cycle. We give the body a chance to express what the intellect often cannot. A soft stretch can become a form of release. A gentle sway can become a way of saying: *I'm here. I feel this. I'm listening.*

In practice, integrating micro-movements into daily life is less about discipline and more about attunement. Begin by building a repertoire of gestures that feel natural and grounding. You might start your day with a brief full-body yawn and reach. You might pause mid-task to roll your ankles or shift your posture. You might notice when your shoulders have crept upward and allow them to drop. The key is *consistency, not complexity*. Over time, these gestures become anchors—predictable returns to self amid unpredictable stimuli.

Importantly, micro-movements also carry an ethical message. In a world that rewards disembodiment—where stillness is mistaken for laziness and rest must be justified—every micro-movement is a subtle act of resistance. It says: *I will not abandon my body to keep pace with your machines*. It says: *Presence matters more than performance*. It says: *My nervous system is not your commodity*.

Ultimately, micro-movements remind us of something that digital life tries to obscure: that the body is not a vehicle to be managed, but a *partner to be heard*. When we treat it with that respect, the shift is not just physical. It is existential. We come back into coherence—not through force, but through care. Not by optimising, but by *noticing*.

This is the quiet genius of micro-movements. They do not demand our attention. They *restore* it. One breath. One stretch. One deliberate pause. And the system begins to reset. Not because it was broken, but because it was finally given space to remember itself.

The Body as the First Technology

Before algorithms, before electricity, before even language as we know it—there was the body. A living, breathing, sensing system designed not just for survival, but for discernment. Long before we outsourced our awareness to digital tools and wearable tech, the body performed complex calculations in real time: assessing threat, registering connection, monitoring internal coherence, and intuitively adjusting to its environment. It was our first dashboard, our original interface. And unlike the cold logic of machines, it offered not only data but *meaning*. The body was—and remains—a sacred technology. But in modern culture, it is a forgotten one.

Today, many people experience their bodies primarily as problems to solve. Something to manage, optimise, tone, correct. The language of biohacking and quantified selfhood has infiltrated even the wellness world, reducing the body to a series of metrics: steps taken, calories burned, sleep cycles completed. Yet none of these measurements capture the intelligence of a gut feeling, the knowing in a heartbeat, or the quiet recalibration that happens when we lie down and *let ourselves feel*. In reducing the body to output, we have stripped it of dignity. Worse, we have silenced its wisdom.

But this wisdom still pulses underneath the noise. It is present when your skin tightens in response to tension in a room, before anyone has said a word. It's alive when your breath shortens as you scroll past something emotionally charged. It's there when your stomach churns at a decision your mind is trying to justify. These are not metaphors. They are *neurological events*—the body detecting, responding, and interpreting its world with a precision no external technology can match.

The somatic disciplines—ranging from trauma-informed therapy to contemplative movement practices—have long understood this. They recognise that the body holds what the mind cannot articulate, and that regulation begins not with thought but with *sensation*. When you close your eyes and feel your feet on the ground, you're not indulging in a moment of relaxation. You're activating your proprioceptive and interoceptive systems—sensory networks that tell you where you are in space, and how you are doing internally.

These systems shape our sense of self. When disrupted, as they are by chronic digital engagement, the result is not just stress, but *disorientation.* You forget what calm feels like because the signals from your own body are drowned out.

This disconnection is not accidental—it is cultural. Western modernity has long prioritised cognition over embodiment, mind over flesh. The result is a subtle but dangerous split: the belief that the body is simply a vehicle for the brain, rather than an intelligent entity in its own right. Digital technology has amplified this split. When we rely on screens to tell us when to move, when to rest, when to eat, we internalise the message that the body cannot be trusted. That it must be managed externally. That it is fundamentally flawed. Over time, this erodes self-trust at the most basic level.

Reframing the body as a sacred technology means rejecting this narrative. It means recognising that the body is not primitive, but *primordial.* Its intelligence is not obsolete; it is foundational. Unlike machines, which operate on binary logic, the body works through rhythm, nuance, and interrelation. It is not simply a sensor—it is a meaning-maker. It doesn't just react. It *remembers.* Trauma, for instance, is stored not in the story we tell about the past, but in the tension patterns of the muscles, the breath-holding reflex, the startle response. Healing comes not just from insight, but from re-establishing a felt sense of safety—through the body.

This has profound implications for how we live in a digitised world. While most solutions to tech overwhelm are framed in terms of screen time limits or productivity tweaks, the real antidote lies deeper: in the *re-inhabiting of our own sensory apparatus.* The ability to listen to one's body—to sense when enough is enough, when presence has faded, when disconnection has set in—is a form of *sovereignty.* It allows us to make choices not from reactivity or external metrics, but from alignment.

This alignment is not static. It is dynamic and responsive. It shifts throughout the day, requiring regular tuning. This is where the metaphor of technology becomes instructive. Just as any sophisticated system requires regular recalibration, so too does the body. But while machines need updates from engineers, the body self-calibrates through *awareness.* A few minutes of breath-focused stillness. A moment of mindful walking. A deep stretch followed by stillness. These are not wellness luxuries. They are maintenance rituals for the most advanced operating system ever developed: the human body.

Importantly, the body's intelligence extends beyond self-regulation. It is also a site of intuition. This is not the "sixth sense" mystified by popular culture, but the *cumulative wisdom of the senses.* It is pattern recognition honed by experience, stored not in language but in nerve endings. When you get a "gut feeling," it is your enteric nervous system—a dense network of neurons in the gut—offering input that has bypassed the linear processing of the prefrontal cortex. This input is often more accurate in complex, uncertain scenarios than conscious reasoning. Yet most people have been trained to override it, to privilege logic over somatic knowing. In doing so, we've lost a vital form of intelligence.

To reclaim the body as the first technology, then, is to reclaim *a different way of knowing.* One that is not always rational, but deeply reliable. One that doesn't speak in words, but in shifts of breath, pulse, posture, and heat. This knowing doesn't compete with cognitive intelligence. It complements it. It grounds it. And in a world increasingly driven by abstraction, data, and disembodied discourse, it becomes more essential—not less.

What might change if we trusted the body's cues as much as we trust digital notifications? What might it mean to structure a day not around the external clock, but around cycles of tension and release, energy and rest, openness and contraction? These questions are not theoretical. They are practical. They invite a return to a form of living that honours our biology rather than constantly overriding it.

This chapter, then, is not an invitation to romanticise the body or reduce it to a self-help trope. It is a call to re-centre it as *a source of truth.* In a world that constantly demands our attention, the body quietly offers us *orientation.* It shows us how we are, what we need, and when we've strayed too far from ourselves. It is not perfect, but it is *precise.* And when we learn to listen—truly listen—we discover that the most sophisticated tool for healing, discerning, and living well has been with us all along. Not in the cloud. Not in the app. But under our skin.

Digital Disembodiment and the Return to Flesh

To speak of screens as merely tools is to miss their deeper cultural significance. They are not neutral devices that passively extend human capability—they are environments that *reshape* how we relate to time, attention, others, and ourselves. And perhaps most profoundly, they are portals through which we exit the body. In a world where much of modern life is mediated through screens, we are witnessing not just a behavioural shift, but a profound ontological one: a gradual drift from *embodied experience* to a digitised form of *disembodied attention.* The cost of this migration is not immediately visible in data points or usage metrics—it is felt in the erosion of presence, the fraying of sensory awareness, and the quiet alienation from our own flesh.

Digital disembodiment is not hyperbole. It is a condition with measurable cognitive and physiological consequences. When we are online, our senses narrow. The eyes dominate, scanning and reacting in a mode of hyper-vigilance. The auditory field is shaped not by ambient, natural sound, but by curated, compressed noise. Touch is replaced with glass. Smell and taste vanish entirely. The proprioceptive sense—the internal map of where we are in space—fades as we sit, often hunched and still, for hours. We are reduced to a pair of eyes and fingers, consuming information without metabolising experience. Over time, the body is rendered peripheral. It becomes an afterthought, something to be 'worked on' at the gym or treated at the spa, rather than inhabited daily as the *primary site of life*.

This disembodiment isn't just physical—it is existential. When we live predominantly in screen-based environments, we unconsciously adopt a flattened sense of being. The interface rewards speed, not depth; reaction, not reflection. Our bodies, by contrast, exist in slow time. They process pain, pleasure, fear, and fatigue in rhythms that do not align with algorithmic urgency. When we privilege screen logic over bodily intelligence, we learn to *mistrust* the body's signals. Hunger is ignored. Fatigue is postponed. Emotional surges are pathologised. We begin to treat our very sensations as interruptions to the productivity machine we are trying to become.

This is not just a personal health issue—it is a cultural crisis. A society disconnected from the body is more easily manipulated, more susceptible to anxiety, more likely to engage in compulsive behaviour. It is less resilient, less capable of discernment, and ultimately less alive. Philosophers like Maurice Merleau-Ponty, who argued that perception is *always embodied*, warned against the mind-body split that Western rationalism normalised. Today, digital technologies have made that split not merely philosophical, but *experiential*. We are learning to live from the neck up, and we are paying for it with our psychological coherence.

What, then, does it mean to *return to flesh*? It means re-rooting ourselves in the sensory field that screens have de-prioritised. It means reclaiming movement not just as exercise, but as communication. It means letting our feet feel the weight of our bodies, letting our breath deepen without instruction, letting our hands encounter texture and temperature without mediation. To return to flesh is to remember that the body is not an inconvenience—it is a compass. It tells us what is true before the mind has time to rationalise. It offers feedback on every relationship, every task, every environment. It doesn't lie. It simply speaks a language we've forgotten how to hear.

This return is not nostalgic—it is necessary. And it begins not with ideology, but with practice. You feel disembodiment most acutely when you contrast it with moments of embodiment. Walking barefoot. Taking a slow bath. Holding eye contact without words. Eating without distraction. These are not luxuries. They are micro-rituals of return. They remind the nervous system that life is *lived*, not streamed. That intimacy is *felt*, not posted. That healing is *relational*, not optimised.

Crucially, returning to flesh is not about rejecting technology—it is about re-establishing *primacy*. The screen can serve us, but it must not replace us. If our identity is being constructed online, our aliveness must be cultivated offline. If the internet is a stage for performance, the body is where authenticity rehearses. And if algorithms are engineered to predict our desires, the body is where *real longing* originates. It is not programmable. It is not replicable. It is a site of mystery, memory, and meaning. And it will not wait forever to be re-inhabited.

There is a reason trauma therapists often say, "The body keeps the score." But it also holds the potential for integration. When we return to the body—fully, consciously—we are not just reducing stress. We are reclaiming agency. We are saying, in effect: *I will not outsource my knowing. I will not dislocate my presence. I will live from the inside out.* This stance is not romantic. It is radical. It disrupts the attention economy at its root. Because a person who is fully in their body cannot be easily seduced by digital noise. They are less likely to scroll past their own needs. They are less likely to perform, posture, or pursue hollow validation. They are already *home.*

The return to flesh is not a one-time act. It is a practice, a discipline, a daily decision to drop out of the hyperreal and re-enter the actual. And the actual is not always comfortable. It includes aches, contradictions, and feelings that cannot be filtered. But it also includes warmth, instinct, and the irreplaceable texture of real life. It includes the thump of your heartbeat in your chest, the rise of your breath as you speak, the subtle current of aliveness that no screen can simulate. And when you learn to trust that current, you find that you no longer need to be constantly connected—because you *are* connected. Not to WiFi, but to your *own existence.*

Let this be the quiet revolution: not logging off in protest, but waking up in your skin. Not escaping the digital, but *remembering the flesh.* Because this body, this breath, this moment—it's not an inconvenience. It's the only place you have ever truly been.

Chapter 6
The Myth of Productivity and the Cult of Busyness

Rewrite the following article to pass AI-detection tools while retaining its professional, intellectually engaging, and authoritative tone.

Rephrase and restructure the content to feel human-authored, with a writing style that reflects the subtle imperfections and expressive flow of a skilled writer.

Specifically: – Vary sentence structures, paragraph rhythms, and transition choices to avoid algorithmic patterns

– Introduce occasional conversational touches or rhetorical asides where appropriate

– Make subtle word choices or phrase shifts that sound natural but aren't statistically predictable

– Avoid "perfectly smooth" sentence-to-sentence transitions—a little friction is more human

– Maintain the original meaning, flow, facts, and paragraphing

– Do not simplify or summarise—this is not a paraphrasing task, but a creative re-authorship

– Use British English conventions

– Ensure the result still reads like it was written by a seasoned nonfiction writer with intellectual and emotional depth

Output only the reworked article text. No explanations. No headers. No setup language.

There was a time—not so long ago—when a person's worth was measured not by their output, but by their integrity, presence, and wisdom. Work had rhythm. Rest had dignity. Slowness was not a flaw in the human operating system, but a feature of life lived in tune with nature's pace. Today, that worldview has collapsed under the weight of an ideology so pervasive it's become invisible: productivity as moral virtue. In this cultural script, to be busy is to be valuable. To be tired is to be trusted. And to be still is to be suspect.

This chapter is an unflinching dissection of that script.

We live in a culture that has turned "doing" into a performance and "being" into a liability. From the way we glorify packed calendars to the guilt we feel when taking an afternoon nap, the signs are clear: busyness is the new badge of honour. The hustle, the grind, the "rise and grind" slogans so casually shared—they all stem from a deeply internalised belief that time must be maximised, monetised, or managed to prove our legitimacy in the world. In the background of every productivity app, every morning routine optimisation, every hacked schedule, is the same underlying message: you are not enough unless you are producing something.

This belief is not benign. It is corrosive. It infiltrates our sleep, our relationships, our breath. It teaches us that if we stop—truly stop—we will fall behind. That there is no inherent worth in being awake to life unless that wakefulness produces measurable results. And so we live in hyperdrive, checking boxes, chasing metrics, addicted to a sense of progress that never quite satisfies. We become so busy managing life that we forget how to experience it.

Part of the illusion is historical. The industrial age ushered in the idea that time was a resource to be sliced, sold, and scheduled. The digital age doubled down, promising that with the right tools, every moment could be made efficient. In reality, what we have created is a culture of chronic acceleration. Even rest is now a performance—tracked, optimised, turned into a metric. We no longer ask, "How do I feel?" but, "How well did my device say I slept?" The line between human being and human capital has blurred to the point of absurdity.

This is not just a lifestyle issue—it is a philosophical crisis. At its core lies a confusion between value and visibility, between essence and performance. We perform productivity to reassure ourselves and others that we belong. But what if belonging never required performance? What if rest was not a break from being valuable, but a return to remembering that we always were?

The deeper question, then, is not how to be more productive—but why we feel compelled to be productive in the first place. What are we avoiding in our frantic motion? What silence are we afraid we might hear if we slowed down long enough to listen? What truths—about our fatigue, our longing, our mortality—have we buried beneath our colour-coded calendars?

This chapter offers no simple answers, because the problem is not simply logistical. It is existential. We are not suffering from poor time management; we are suffering from misplaced meaning. Somewhere along the way, we confused motion with purpose. We mistook accumulation for fulfilment. We started treating time as an enemy to conquer rather than a sacred rhythm to align with.

But if time can be misused, it can also be reclaimed. And here lies the promise of reorientation. When we begin to see time not as a commodity, but as a spiritual resource—one that reflects our attention, our choices, our values—everything changes. We stop asking how much we can squeeze into a day and start asking what truly deserves our presence. We begin to honour the arc of natural cycles—expansion and contraction, effort and integration—rather than fighting against them in pursuit of perpetual output.

Slowness, then, is not laziness. It is discernment. And rest is not indulgence. It is recovery of self. To surrender to a slower rhythm is not to give up—it is to realign with the pace at which depth, wisdom, and embodiment can emerge. Nature does not bloom year-round. Neither do we. Yet digital culture pretends otherwise, encouraging a form of pseudo-mastery that leaves the soul threadbare.

This chapter also explores the psychological impact of optimisation culture. The compulsion to track every habit, maximise every minute, and "hack" even our healing practices reflects a deep distrust of our organic intelligence. It treats the body not as an ecosystem, but as a machine. But healing does not respond to coercion. It responds to permission—to be slow, to be messy, to unfold in nonlinear time. By re-humanising our relationship to productivity, we begin to reclaim that permission.

You will also be invited to examine the cultural narratives that link self-worth to output—especially in work, parenting, and creative expression. How many of us feel ashamed when we're not "achieving"? How often do we over-explain or apologise for rest? What if those moments of presence—the kind that go undocumented, unnoticed, unmeasured—were actually the most meaningful? What if being deeply present with a child, a tree, or one's own breath was the highest expression of value?

Finally, this chapter gestures toward an alternative paradigm: cyclical living. Inspired by seasonal wisdom and ancient rhythms, cyclical living honours the truth that all life moves in waves. There are times for focus and times for flux, times for striving and times for stillness. When we orient ourselves to these rhythms—biological, planetary, emotional—we begin to cultivate a life that is not just sustainable, but soulful.

You will not find five quick tips to escape burnout here. Instead, you will be asked to sit with uncomfortable questions, to challenge internalised scripts, and to consider a deeper form of productivity—one measured not in speed, but in depth of contact with life. Because the real myth is not that we need to do more. The real myth is that doing more will save us.

To dismantle this myth is not to reject ambition, discipline, or creativity. It is to reimagine them through the lens of presence. It is to honour that your being is not a performance. And it is to remember that the most powerful form of rebellion in a culture addicted to doing is this: to simply be. Not efficiently. Not visibly. But wholly, quietly, and without apology.

Let us begin.

How Productivity Became a Proxy for Worth

Productivity, once a neutral descriptor of output, has quietly transformed into something far more insidious: a moral yardstick. The modern individual is not merely evaluated by what they contribute, but by how *efficiently* and *unceasingly* they contribute. This isn't about work alone—it's about identity. In many professional and cultural spaces today, to be seen as successful, respectable, or even *good*, one must be demonstrably busy. Busyness, far from being a symptom of imbalance, is now flaunted as a signal of value. And lurking just beneath this cultural script is a deeply corrosive belief: if you're not producing, you're not enough.

This is not a natural state of affairs. It is the result of a slow, centuries-long accretion of ideas, many of which are more political and economic than they are rational or ethical. Tracing this phenomenon requires more than pointing to the daily grind of modern life; it involves interrogating the historical forces that yoked personal virtue to output, and the psychological toll of internalising this linkage.

One cannot disentangle the cult of productivity from its roots in the Industrial Revolution, which inaugurated a mechanistic view of the human being. Time became standardised. Labour became segmented. People were no longer artisans or stewards of cyclical, seasonal rhythms—they were *workers* in the strictest sense, expected to conform to clocks, quotas, and the relentless logic of efficiency. Worth shifted from *being* to *doing*, and from doing to *producing at scale*. Even rest was repurposed as fuel for further labour, not an end in itself.

The Protestant work ethic played a pivotal role in moralising this framework. Calvinist theology in particular cast hard work not merely as necessary, but as evidence of divine favour. To be idle was to invite spiritual decay. In this worldview, rest was permissible only if it enhanced future productivity, and material success became an outward marker of moral virtue. These ideas, embedded in the bones of capitalist societies, have outlived their theological origins. Today, they persist not through sermons, but through LinkedIn posts, time-tracking apps, and a thousand small ways we compare ourselves to those who seem to be doing *more.*

In contemporary life, especially in the digital economy, this linkage has metastasised. Consider how the smartphone collapses boundaries between work and rest. The office follows you into your bedroom. Emails become a 24-hour drip-feed. Even leisure time is colonised by a compulsion to *optimise*—whether it's tracking your sleep, gamifying your workouts, or turning your weekend hobbies into monetisable side projects. Productivity is no longer confined to the workplace; it has become a totalising ethos, shaping how we move, eat, parent, rest, and even heal.

The result is an epidemic of internalised shame. People feel guilty for taking a day off. They apologise for sleeping in. They call time with family "unproductive" as though human connection were somehow extraneous to the business of life. This is not simply about overwork; it's about *identity distortion.* When worth is measured in terms of constant output, rest becomes *laziness*, presence becomes *indulgence*, and self-worth becomes *conditional.* The nervous system, flooded with cortisol, forgets what it means to feel safe without a task to perform. The soul, meanwhile, grows threadbare—visible only when reflected in metrics, performance reviews, or external praise.

Critically, the internalisation of productivity as worth is not experienced equally. Marginalised communities, especially women and people of colour, often feel a double burden: not only must they produce to earn validation, but they must outperform to even be perceived as equal. For those whose existence is already questioned or undervalued, the pressure to *prove* their worth through relentless doing becomes doubly acute. And in this framework, those unable to produce—due to illness, disability, age, or care responsibilities—are quietly marginalised or rendered invisible.

The psychological fallout is profound. Burnout is no longer an occupational hazard; it is a cultural condition. Rates of anxiety, depression, and exhaustion are not aberrations—they are symptoms of a society that has forgotten how to honour stillness. But more insidiously, this system gaslights us into believing that the problem lies *within*. If we're overwhelmed, we must not be managing our time well. If we're exhausted, we must need better "self-care routines." The solution is always more effort, more structure, more performance. The system that creates the exhaustion never questions itself—it only sells us productivity tools to cope with it.

The antidote is not simple. It requires a redefinition of value—one that decouples worth from output and dares to assert that being *fully human* is valuable in itself. This means embracing the radical idea that rest is *necessary*, not because it makes us more productive, but because it makes us more whole. It means reclaiming presence as a form of resistance, not retreat. And it means recognising that the most profound forms of value—empathy, creativity, connection, wisdom—cannot be mass-produced, optimised, or monetised.

A mother cradling her child in a quiet room is not less worthy than a founder scaling a tech startup. A man lying under a tree watching clouds is not less successful than one closing a seven-figure deal. A person navigating chronic illness is not failing at life because their body cannot "perform" like others. These truths must be remembered, not because they sound noble, but because forgetting them has real-world consequences: disconnection, alienation, and a culture in which no one can ever quite rest without guilt.

We must ask better questions. Not "What did I get done today?" but "Was I present for what mattered?" Not "Did I earn my rest?" but "Did I allow myself to be human?" These are not soft questions. They are revolutionary. They challenge the very metrics by which we have been taught to measure ourselves. They demand a shift from proving to *belonging*, from performance to *presence*.

And if we are to reclaim our lives from the cult of busyness, we must begin here: by dismantling the lie that our worth must be earned through doing. By remembering that our value was never up for debate. And by stepping back into the radical, restorative truth that being—fully, consciously, unapologetically—is not a luxury. It is our birthright.

Doing vs. Being: The Existential Crisis

Modern life does not reward being. It rewards doing—publicly, constantly, and visibly. From the moment we wake, we are pulled into a momentum not of our own making: checking emails, scanning newsfeeds, responding to messages, updating calendars, tracking steps. We don't so much inhabit our lives as perform them. Every action, down to the most mundane, is now accompanied by a subtle undertone of surveillance, metrics, and comparison. In such a world, doing is not merely activity—it becomes identity. And being? Being becomes a luxury we believe we must first *earn*.

The existential toll of this shift is profound, yet difficult to articulate. What we're facing is not simply burnout or fatigue. It's something more elemental—a growing disconnection from our essence. A fraying of the quiet, interior sense of self that once existed independently of output, validation, or productivity. The question is no longer "What am I becoming?" but "What have I forgotten to be?"

To understand how we got here, we must trace the subtle but decisive shift from existential presence to performative existence. The digital world didn't invent this dynamic, but it accelerated it to a point of near-total saturation. Historically, being—conscious awareness, interiority, contemplative aliveness—was seen as a source of wisdom. Whether in ancient philosophical traditions or contemplative spiritual paths, stillness was honoured as fertile ground for insight. In contrast, modernity has recast stillness as suspect. To be still is to risk being seen as unproductive. To be contemplative is to risk being labelled disengaged. In a world that overvalues performance, being slips into irrelevance.

The mechanisms of digital life are not neutral in this transformation. The architecture of social media, the rise of personal branding, the incessant pressure to prove one's life is interesting, meaningful, and productive—all contribute to a culture of *existence-as-exhibition*. Our identities, once grounded in community, land, ritual, or silence, are now curated, edited, and optimised for visibility. We are encouraged to think of ourselves not as people but as *projects*: to track, upgrade, brand, and monetise. Even moments of supposed rest are captured, filtered, and shared—not as experiences to be lived, but as proof that we are still participating in the great productivity theatre.

This pressure is not only external. Over time, it becomes internalised. The inner monologue changes. Stillness begins to feel like guilt. Doing nothing becomes synonymous with being nothing. The moment we pause, we feel a need to justify it—to ourselves, to others, to the invisible audience we've built in our minds. What began as a cultural current becomes a personal anxiety: "Am I falling behind?" "Should I be doing more?" "What does this say about me?"

The result is an epidemic of existential shallowness. When doing eclipses being, depth disappears. The silence in which we once found clarity is now filled with noise. The solitude in which we once rediscovered ourselves is now avoided like a threat. The question "Who am I?" becomes harder to answer when we are never alone long enough to ask it without an audience.

Yet the irony is that all our doing, though incessant, is not making us more fulfilled. If anything, it is hollowing us out. Rates of anxiety and depression continue to climb, even among the most professionally "successful." People speak of feeling adrift, scattered, dislocated—not because they lack activity, but because they lack *alignment*. They are doing more than ever, but no longer know why.

The soul, if spoken of at all, is reduced to a weekend retreat or a line in a bio. Essence has been traded for execution.

And yet, the hunger for being has not disappeared. It waits—often just beneath the surface of exhaustion, cynicism, or performance fatigue. It shows up in those unexpected moments when the algorithm loses its grip: a walk without a podcast, an afternoon nap without guilt, an hour in conversation where time vanishes. It shows up when we catch ourselves longing for something we cannot quite name—something slower, quieter, more real.

Reclaiming being, then, is not about withdrawing from life. It is about re-entering life differently. It is about cultivating spaces where worth is not measured, where presence is not performed, where aliveness is not instrumentalised. This doesn't require abandoning our roles or ambitions. It requires *reframing* them. Instead of asking how much we can do, we must ask what is worth doing—and what version of ourselves is showing up to do it.

To do this, we must create boundaries around our attention. Not simply to avoid distraction, but to protect the soil in which being can take root. We must resist the reflex to optimise every hour, every experience, every interaction. Not everything needs to be a stepping stone. Some things—most things—are valuable simply because they are. The laughter of a friend, the quiet of a morning, the rhythm of the breath—these are not interruptions to doing. They are reminders of *being*.

This shift also calls for new language. We must become suspicious of the terms that colonise our self-concept: hustle, grind, scale, growth. We must learn to speak again of presence, spaciousness, rhythm, depth. We must teach our children not just how to achieve, but how to listen. Not just how to build, but how to *become*.

At a collective level, the implications are immense. Cultures that privilege doing over being produce burnout, not brilliance. They foster comparison, not connection. They glorify speed, but often at the cost of wisdom. What would it mean to build systems—educational, organisational, social—that honour *both* action and awareness? What would it mean to design technologies that nourish being rather than merely reward doing?

None of this is easy. Being requires courage. It often means standing still while the world rushes past. It means tolerating discomfort, ambiguity, even boredom—states that digital life has taught us to avoid. But it is in that very discomfort that we rediscover our humanity. When we stop doing long enough to feel, we remember what it is to be alive—not as a role, but as a presence. Not as a brand, but as a *soul.*

Ultimately, this existential crisis is not a flaw in the system. It is a signal. A call to recalibrate our lives away from the tyranny of constant doing and back toward the dignity of simply being. Not because it is more "efficient" or "productive" (though paradoxically, it often is), but because it is *true.* Because doing without being is hollow. And because we were not born to prove ourselves. We were born to *be ourselves.*

The Tyranny of Efficiency

Efficiency, once a principle of intelligent design and economic prudence, has been exalted into a modern deity. Its creed echoes across boardrooms, classrooms, and meditation apps alike: *do more, faster, with less friction.* But what happens when a culture obsessed with optimisation applies the same logic to the human soul? When the messy, nonlinear process of healing is measured by productivity metrics? When our need for stillness is pathologised as inefficiency? The tyranny of efficiency is not just a productivity problem—it's a philosophical rupture in our understanding of what it means to be well, whole, and human.

At the heart of this phenomenon lies hustle culture, a set of values that frames unrelenting effort as virtue. It does not merely encourage hard work—it glorifies exhaustion. Sleep becomes optional. Rest is reframed as guilt. Leisure is granted only if it serves a larger goal. And in this worldview, there are no natural endpoints—just plateaus to optimise, habits to hack, and baselines to beat. The tyranny comes not from the desire to improve, but from the inability to *stop* improving. Every moment is a potential input in a lifelong algorithm of self-optimisation.

This mindset has infiltrated not only our work but our wellbeing. The language of hacking, borrowed from computer science, has colonised the wellness world. We now "biohack" our sleep cycles, "neurohack" our habits, and track heart rate variability to monitor stress. It is not that these tools lack value. The problem is the framing. When healing becomes something to optimise, the underlying message is that slowness, messiness, and vulnerability are errors in the code. We come to see emotions as glitches, fatigue as a bug, and setbacks as system failures. This mechanised view of human experience may provide a comforting illusion of control, but it erodes our capacity for self-compassion.

Efficiency's most insidious impact, however, is existential. It reconfigures our relationship with time itself. No longer something to inhabit, time becomes something to *conquer*. The goal is not to feel time, but to compress it. Calendars are overstuffed. Multitasking is valorised. Even recovery must prove its worth—scheduled, tracked, and "stacked" with productive intention. A walk must double as a podcast opportunity. A morning routine must be A/B tested. We are not allowed to *just* be.

What gets lost in this regime of constant calibration is precisely what makes life meaningful: the unquantifiable, the unpredictable, the slow-burning. Deep relationships, creative breakthroughs, and emotional growth do not yield to optimisation. They require inefficiency. They require repetition, silence, boredom, regression, and waiting. And most of all, they require the one thing hustle culture cannot tolerate—*time without agenda.*

The historical roots of this problem run deep. The Industrial Revolution gave rise to the clock as the ultimate symbol of order and productivity. Taylorism and scientific management in the 20th century further enshrined time-efficiency as the gold standard of progress. Today's digital tools are merely an evolution of that legacy—only now, the factory lives in our pocket. Algorithms feed us ever more efficient dopamine loops. Task managers nudge us toward constant activity. Apps reward streaks, not depth. Even meditation is gamified, measured by minutes logged and streaks preserved. We are no longer just working efficiently—we are *living* efficiently. Or trying to.

The result is a chronic state of anticipatory tension. We are always leaning forward, anticipating the next task, the next improvement, the next "level up." This forward tilt disconnects us from the embodied present. We eat quickly, speak quickly, sleep shallowly. Our nervous systems mirror the tempo of our technology: fast, fragmented, and overstimulated. Efficiency becomes a rhythm, but it is a rhythm incompatible with rest.

And this has moral consequences. When we expect ourselves to function as machines, we begin to treat others that way too. Compassion collapses into performance coaching. Grief is allotted a week of paid leave. Parenthood is turned into a sequence of developmental milestones. The messier dimensions of human experience are subtly shamed—unless they can be fixed, measured, or expedited. Vulnerability, once a portal to connection, is rebranded as inefficiency. The soul becomes a throughput problem.

But there is an alternative. What if we reframed inefficiency not as failure, but as fidelity—to the deeper rhythms of life, to the needs of the body, to the wisdom of pause? What if instead of hacking healing, we honoured it as sacred space? What if we let go of the fantasy of frictionless living and remembered that friction is where growth often begins?

In practice, this requires both inner and outer resistance. Internally, we must notice how quickly we judge ourselves in moments of pause: the twitch to check email while waiting in line, the unease of sitting still, the compulsion to optimise every hobby. That discomfort is not a sign of laziness—it is the residue of a culture that equates being with idling and rest with irrelevance. Learning to resist that impulse is a radical act of reclamation.

Externally, it means protecting pockets of life that do not serve a productive end. Long meals. Wandering conversations. Unstructured play. Journaling with no agenda. Resting with no justification. These are not luxuries—they are essential nutrients for a soul starved of slowness.

It also requires rethinking leadership and culture. In the workplace, valuing deep work over visible busyness. In education, prioritising curiosity over rote achievement. In healthcare, remembering that healing is not linear. These shifts are not merely strategic—they are ethical. They represent a refusal to let human life be flattened into throughput.

To be clear, efficiency has its place. No one is advocating chaos. But when it becomes the master narrative of our lives, it crowds out everything that cannot be measured—wonder, intimacy, slowness, reverence. These are not inefficiencies. They are the *ends* of life, not its waste.

So the next time you find yourself reaching for another optimisation, another shortcut, another hack, pause. Ask: What am I trying to save? And at what cost? In a culture that treats every moment as a means to something else, choosing to be inefficient is not laziness. It is *liberation.*

Because ultimately, a meaningful life is not one that runs the smoothest. It is one that *matters*. And meaning does not come from how efficiently we pass through life—but how deeply we inhabit it.

Time as a Spiritual Resource

We live in a culture that treats time as both enemy and currency. It is "spent," "wasted," "managed," "crunched," "saved," and "killed." These metaphors betray a transactional, adversarial relationship with the most finite of human resources. Time, in the modern vernacular, is something to control. But what if it were something to *honour* instead? What if time was not simply a logistical problem to solve, but a spiritual dimension to dwell in—one that reflects our deepest values, shapes our inner landscape, and defines how fully we are able to inhabit our lives?

To approach time as a spiritual resource is not to indulge in mysticism or abandon practicality. It is to engage in a deliberate reorientation—away from seeing hours as units of output, and toward recognising them as containers of meaning. Time is not just the medium in which life unfolds. It is life itself. And how we engage with it is among the most profound expressions of who we are.

This reorientation begins by acknowledging the dominant cultural narrative that defines worth in terms of productivity. Our tools and technologies are optimised to make us faster, more efficient, and more available. Calendar apps fragment our attention into coloured blocks. Notifications create micro-disruptions throughout the day, forcing us into a pattern of compulsive checking and task-switching. The very design of digital life promotes immediacy over depth, acceleration over presence. In this paradigm, time is not sacred—it is something to be conquered.

But the spiritual traditions of the world have long offered an alternative lens. In contemplative Christianity, the Sabbath is a consecrated interruption of work—a weekly reminder that existence is enough. In Buddhist mindfulness, the breath anchors us to *now*, the only moment that truly exists. Indigenous worldviews often view time not as linear and extractive, but as cyclical and relational—a rhythm to be tuned into, not a commodity to exploit. These traditions, diverse though they are, converge on a central insight: *how we hold time is how we hold life.*

When we rush through time, we rush through ourselves. We skip over sensations, cut short conversations, and abandon reflection. Slowness becomes a liability, presence a luxury. But in the process, we sever our access to the richness that makes life worth living. Gratitude, awe, intimacy—these are not instantaneous experiences. They require space. They require attention. And they require a pace of being that digital culture increasingly renders alien.

The psychological toll of this disconnection is not abstract. Chronic time-scarcity is one of the most consistent predictors of stress and anxiety in modern populations. When individuals feel they don't have "enough time," they report lower levels of happiness, diminished capacity for empathy, and a greater tendency to make impulsive decisions. Scarcity mindsets, especially around time, push the nervous system into a constant state of mild threat—perceiving life as a series of obligations rather than opportunities for meaning.

By contrast, those who cultivate what psychologists call "time affluence"—a subjective sense of having enough time—tend to experience higher well-being, better relationships, and increased creativity. Time affluence is not about wealth or freedom from responsibility. It is a perceptual shift rooted in how one *relates* to time. It is a function of internal spaciousness rather than external schedule.

One way to reclaim this spaciousness is to become more intentional about the rhythms that govern our days. Most of us operate under a flattened chronology: one task follows another in an undifferentiated blur. But human beings are rhythmic creatures. Our bodies move in circadian cycles. Our minds fluctuate between focus and rest. Even our emotions have their own tidal movements. When we ignore these rhythms in the name of efficiency, we become unmoored. But when we design our time to reflect the pulse of nature and psyche alike—incorporating moments of stillness, deep work, social connection, and solitude—we restore coherence to our lives.

A useful practice here is the framing of time not in terms of hours and minutes, but in terms of *energy* and *attention.* Ask not just "What will I do today?" but "What deserves my most present self?" This is the beginning of a spiritual economy: one in which time is not allocated based on urgency, but based on alignment.

Such an economy requires boundaries. A spiritually mature relationship with time is impossible without the courage to say *no.* No to commitments that dilute our presence. No to technologies that extract more than they offer. No to the internalised voice that equates stillness with failure. In its place, we say yes to fewer, deeper things. We trade breadth for depth, speed for resonance. This is not a rejection of ambition or a prescription for monastic withdrawal. It is a redirection of energy toward that which sustains our humanity.

It also demands a reimagination of endings. Much of our anxiety around time stems from the pressure to "make the most of it"—to squeeze value out of every second. This impulse, while understandable, often leads to a subtle form of existential panic. But when we honour time as sacred, we learn to meet endings not with grasping, but with gratitude. A walk ends. A conversation concludes. A season passes. And in each case, the closing is not a diminishment, but a completion. Presence, not prolongation, becomes the goal.

Modern attempts to master time through productivity tools, performance metrics, and habit-stacking have their place. But they are incomplete without a deeper foundation. That foundation is reverence. When we treat time as sacred, we begin to *attune* rather than *optimise.* We become less obsessed with the passage of time and more attuned to its *quality*—its texture, its flavour, its emotional resonance. A single hour can feel either dense with meaning or utterly hollow. The difference lies in how we show up to it.

This perspective has powerful implications not just for individual wellbeing, but for collective culture. Imagine workplaces that structured time around human flourishing, not just output. Imagine schools that respected the slow unfolding of attention. Imagine families who valued presence over performance. These shifts are not utopian—they are urgent. And they begin with a redefinition of time itself.

Time is not neutral. It reflects and reinforces what we hold sacred. The way we design, distribute, and dwell in time tells the truth about our values—more clearly, perhaps, than our words ever could. If we wish to live lives of depth and meaning, we must ask not just *how* we spend our time, but *why*. And we must be willing to let that answer shape our days.

Because ultimately, time is not just something we *have*. It is something we *become*. The hours we give our presence to shape our identity, our relationships, and our legacy. When we honour time, we honour life itself. And in doing so, we create a space where the sacred is not some distant abstraction, but something unfolding in real time—moment by moment, breath by breath.

Surrendering to the Slow Rhythm

Modern life operates on an artificial tempo. Our devices refresh in milliseconds, our inboxes demand responses in minutes, and our calendars are sliced into half-hour segments like parcels in a conveyor belt. Even rest has been commodified: "biohack your sleep," "optimise your recovery," "meditate for productivity." Speed is no longer merely a by-product of technological innovation—it has become a doctrine. The result is a kind of quiet devastation: a human nervous system strained by perpetual urgency, a culture alienated from depth, and a psyche that confuses acceleration with advancement.

But there is another rhythm available to us—one that existed long before digital clocks and dopamine loops. It is the rhythm of the seasons, of the moon, of our breath, our circadian pulses, and our emotional tides. It is the rhythm of nature. And in remembering it, we are offered not just relief, but restoration. *To surrender to the slow rhythm is not to withdraw from life, but to finally begin living in alignment with it.*

The concept of cyclical living is not new. Indigenous cultures, traditional agricultural societies, and even ancient philosophers understood that life unfolds in patterns—waxing and waning, blooming and composting, inhaling and exhaling. Time was not a line to race along, but a circle to move with. There were seasons for growth and seasons for rest; phases of visibility and phases of retreat. Nature did not apologise for winter. It did not resent the dormancy of soil or the long hush before spring.

Contrast this with the prevailing ethos of today, where slowing down is often pathologised. We praise those who "grind," who "hustle," who "maximise." Slowness is perceived as inefficient, regressive, or indulgent. Yet this relentless tempo is neither sustainable nor natural. Physiologically, the human body is not designed for unbroken output. Our hormonal systems require downregulation. Our creativity needs incubation. Our relationships need time that is not fractured by screens or overshadowed by agendas. In other words, we are biological creatures trying to keep pace with a mechanical world—and the friction is costing us dearly.

The cost is measurable. Burnout is no longer a fringe concern of high-powered executives—it is endemic, affecting students, caregivers, freelancers, and factory workers alike. Anxiety and sleep disorders are surging. Attention spans are shrinking. Across demographics, there is a growing sense that people are *moving faster but arriving nowhere*. The deeper tragedy is that many have internalised this speed as a moral imperative. To slow down feels shameful. To rest feels undeserved. We do not need more productivity tools—we need a new metaphor for time.

Cyclical living offers this metaphor. It invites us to think seasonally rather than sequentially, to honour ebb as much as flow. Instead of asking "How much can I get done today?" we might ask "What season am I in right now—and what does it call for?" Am I in a spring of ideation, or a winter of quiet integration? Is this a moment to initiate or to reflect, to speak or to listen, to push or to pause?

This approach is not about romanticising nature or rejecting structure. It's about recalibrating to a pace that honours the body, the psyche, and the soul. It's about replacing the tyranny of optimisation with the wisdom of rhythm. When we align our lifestyle with these rhythms, everything changes: our expectations, our boundaries, even our sense of worth.

Take work, for instance. Under linear time, the expectation is constant output. Every day must be as productive as the last. Every quarter must beat the previous one. But under cyclical time, productivity waxes and wanes. There are fertile phases, and there are fallow ones. Creativity emerges not just from intense focus, but from spaciousness, from boredom, from wandering thought. Thomas Edison took long walks. Maya Angelou insisted on daily solitude. Beethoven composed outdoors. These weren't indulgences—they were rituals of rhythm, attuned to the needs of their inner ecosystem.

Or consider relationships. In the digital age, connection is incessant but shallow—likes, replies, emojis, updates. We're in contact constantly, yet intimacy suffers. Slowing down invites a different quality of presence. A long meal with no phone in sight. A walk without a destination. A conversation without multitasking. These are not luxuries. They are the conditions in which genuine human connection can occur.

Even healing follows its own cadence. The body doesn't regenerate on command. Emotional wounds do not resolve on a schedule. Yet we are taught to treat recovery like a checklist. "Feel better faster." "Bounce back stronger." "Get over it." But grief, trauma, and transformation do not obey metrics. They move in cycles. They return in waves. They require patience. And they demand our willingness to *be with* what is, not just rush toward what's next.

To live cyclically is also to make peace with mystery. The linear mindset is obsessed with clarity, finality, progress. But real life is often ambiguous, recursive, and nonlinear. Ideas take time to germinate. Clarity arises after confusion. Breakthroughs arrive when we least expect them—often not by speeding up, but by slowing down enough to hear the whisper beneath the noise.

Practically, how does one begin to surrender to the slow rhythm in a culture built on acceleration?

Start with the body. Wake and sleep with the sun. Eat when you're hungry, not when the clock says so. Let your breathing slow. Notice your energy throughout the day—when are you most creative, most focused, most tired? Structure your tasks accordingly, not by artificial standards but by embodied awareness.

Reclaim rituals. Morning pages. Evening tea. Weekly walks. These are not mere habits; they are temporal anchors. They remind you that not every moment must be "used"—some are meant to be *inhabited.* Let your rituals be spacious, sensual, unhurried.

Embrace seasonality in your planning. What if you thought in quarters the way farmers do? What if you took a creative winter, a professional spring, a relational summer, a reflective autumn? What if your calendar reflected your humanity, not just your ambition?

Finally, resist the urge to *justify* slowness. It doesn't need to make you more productive, more creative, or more resilient—though it might. It is enough that it makes you *more alive.*

The invitation here is not to abandon your responsibilities, but to transform your relationship with time itself. To stop treating life as a sprint and start honouring it as a cycle. To surrender is not to give up—it is to give *in* to something wiser than the algorithm, gentler than the metric, truer than the clock.

Because beneath all the noise, the body remembers how to live slowly. The breath remembers. The heart remembers. The earth beneath your feet remembers. The question is—*will you let yourself remember too?*

Chapter 7
The Inner Landscape Reclaimed

A subtle crisis is quietly unfolding—not with spectacle or alarm, but through a slow erosion of the self. What we're witnessing is a diminishing of the inner life: attention thinned to fragments, emotions flattened to reactions, instinct dulled to silence. Where once the psyche was regarded as a sacred, expansive ground—a realm for reflection, intuition, and imaginative depth—it is now increasingly handed over to the digital domain. Apps do the remembering, algorithms do the sorting. We scroll instead of ponder. We respond rather than reflect. We consume so voraciously that we forget to truly feel. And in this unexamined exchange, many have become estranged from the most essential guide they possess: their own interior knowing.

This chapter offers neither complaint nor nostalgia—it is a quiet invitation. Not to retreat from the world, but to return to the self with care and deliberation. It is a call to reclaim the contours of one's inner life, not as some indulgent luxury, but as a vital act of psychological autonomy. Because in a society that thrives on our divided attention and benefits from our emotional disconnection, recovering our interior ground is not merely healing—it is an act of quiet defiance.

Contemporary culture rarely encourages us to take our inner worlds seriously. Reflection is often seen as a delay tactic, stillness mistaken for stagnation. Emotional depth? Only welcomed when it can be neatly packaged or commodified. Even self-awareness has been appropriated, folded into the language of life hacks and performance gains. But flourishing as a human being is about more than being productive. It demands depth—the courage to pause, to sense, to interpret our experience in a way that outstrips metrics or external praise.

The first terrain this chapter charts is the cultivation of space—internal spaciousness—for reflection. As the world continues to compress our attention into soundbites and push-notifications, we must learn to resist that squeeze. This section offers practices not of escape, but of expansion. Think of them as portals rather than pastimes: structured reflection prompts, intentional silence, visualisation work. These are methods that help us digest our lives, anchor in something slower and truer, and become aware of the stories we're living. Without such space, we simply echo the culture around us. With it, we begin to author something of our own.

Central to this process is the practice of sacred journaling. Not the kind used to track goals or optimise mornings. But the kind that emerges when pen meets page as a daily ritual—an exhalation of the soul. Reflective writing, when approached with sincerity, becomes something more than a record. It becomes a mirror, a method of clearing out inner static, a private encounter with what we truly believe and desire. In a world obsessed with being seen, the blank page is where we can be honest without needing to perform.

But what good is writing if one no longer knows how to feel? This is where emotional literacy steps in. Our digital environment has not only hijacked attention; it has also dulled our emotional range. We're overstimulated yet underconnected. Alerts jar us. Comments inflame us. Perfected online lives make us feel somehow less. And so the need arises—to relearn the emotional language that helps us interpret and inhabit our own inner landscape. This chapter returns to that work: differentiating between anticipation and anxiety, or between sadness and the deep, human need to grieve. Without this fluency, our emotional lives become opaque even to us.

Tied closely to emotional literacy is the gentle reawakening of intuition. Frequently dismissed as vague or irrational, intuition is in fact a form of intelligence rooted in the body, in pattern, in presence. It is not noisy. It does not beg to be heard. But it is profoundly trustworthy—if we can quiet ourselves enough to notice it. Yet in a culture of overstimulation, intuition often goes unheard. The nervous system locked in urgency, the mind scattered across a dozen tabs—this is not fertile ground for inner knowing. Here, you'll find gentle practices to reattune the senses, slow the mental machinery, and create space for intuitive guidance to emerge. The less cluttered our inner environment, the more clearly our inner voice can speak.

Which brings us to a humble yet transformative habit: the daily self-check-in. Like checking the weather before stepping out, this practice asks us to check the climate within. What's the emotional tone today? What thought loops are running beneath the surface? What needs expression, or perhaps silence? These brief pauses—whether through breathwork before work, a question scribbled in the margins at dusk, or a moment of somatic presence—anchor us. They don't pull us into self-obsession; rather, they root us in coherence amid a world splintered by speed.

Together, these practices offer more than mindfulness as a slogan. They offer a return to the full range of what it means to be human. They remind us that our thoughts, feelings, and intuitions matter—not because they're profitable, but because they're ours. Because without attention to our interiority, we leave ourselves vulnerable—to manipulation, to exhaustion, to disconnection. Meaning is not found in metrics. It arises in the quiet, in the pause, in the act of paying attention to what stirs beneath the surface.

Reclaiming the inner life is not about endless introspection. It's about building the capacity to show up—to life, to others, to one's own truth—with clarity and depth. This chapter does not offer to fix you. It offers you back to yourself. And in doing so, it readies you to engage the outer world not with performance or panic, but with presence.

Because what we recover within, we carry outward—with more integrity, more empathy, and perhaps—most radically—with a little more truth.

Creating Internal Space for Reflection

We live in an age where silence feels suspicious and slowness is treated as a defect. Thoughtfulness, once considered a virtue, is now often pathologised as procrastination. Reflection—true, sustained, undistracted reflection—is increasingly rare, not because we lack the time for it, but because we have normalised its absence. In a culture engineered for constant stimulus and instantaneous response, internal space has become not only undervalued, but largely unfamiliar. And yet, this space is essential. Not as a retreat from reality, but as the crucible in which clarity, integrity, and meaning are formed.

This article is not about mindfulness in the abstract or meditation as a lifestyle trend. It is a call to carve out *deliberate interior space*—the kind that allows us to pause before reacting, feel before numbing, and examine our lives before automating them. Such space is not merely therapeutic; it is foundational to being fully human. Without it, we become reactive rather than reflective, fragmented rather than integrated, and performative rather than authentic.

The modern nervous system is saturated. Information arrives faster than we can process it. The average person checks their phone hundreds of times a day, each glance a micro-fracture in the continuity of thought. The result is a psychological state that mimics attention while systematically destroying it. Reflection, by contrast, requires slowness. It demands the kind of psychological spaciousness that cannot be achieved between notifications or squeezed into the margins of multitasking. It must be cultivated consciously, and it must be defended—because nothing in the dominant culture will encourage it.

To create internal space for reflection is not to indulge in sentimentality. It is to reintroduce intentionality into a life that may have become defined by speed and surface. This space becomes the place where inner contradictions are reconciled, where intuition is heard beneath the noise, where decisions are anchored not in habit but in clarity. It is here that we remember who we are when we are not performing, producing, or being perceived.

But how does one *build* such a space in a world that demands constant visibility and engagement?

One method is through **structured prompts**—deliberate questions designed not to elicit immediate answers but to provoke sustained inquiry. Prompts are powerful precisely because they disrupt the autopilot. A well-crafted prompt—*What am I avoiding by staying busy?* or *What would I say no to if I truly valued peace?*—can reroute the entire current of awareness. These questions do not belong to the "how-to" genre of self-help. They are invitations into complexity, ambiguity, and inner listening. When returned to regularly, they form the scaffolding for a life examined rather than performed.

Another pathway is through **silence retreats**—structured periods of intentional quiet, whether for an hour, a day, or a week. Silence, in this context, is not simply the absence of sound. It is the intentional removal of *external inputs* so that internal signals can be perceived. Most people associate silence with boredom or awkwardness because they have never spent long enough in it to experience what lies beyond the initial discomfort. But once that threshold is crossed, silence reveals itself as fertile ground. It does not erase thought; it refines it. It does not suppress emotion; it gives it contour. Silence retreats—whether formal or self-created—offer a profound reset not because they provide answers, but because they restore access to questions we've been too busy to ask.

Equally potent is the practice of **visualisation journeys**—guided or self-directed inner explorations that allow symbolic, subconscious, or intuitive insights to surface. Unlike logical analysis, which is linear and language-bound, visualisation speaks to the deeper architecture of the mind: imagery, archetype, emotion. When practised with skill and sincerity, visualisation becomes a bridge between the conceptual and the visceral. It enables us to *feel* what we often only *think*. For example, visualising the "future self" in a space of emotional congruence—safe, purposeful, aligned—can reveal what our current habits and decisions are helping or hindering. Likewise, visualising unresolved parts of the psyche can bring compassion and integration to inner conflicts. These journeys are not escapes from reality; they are rehearsals for living it with more depth and coherence.

It is important to note that creating reflective space is not always comfortable. The first thing that often surfaces in silence is not serenity but *unprocessed noise.* Anxieties we've been outrunning. Feelings we've suppressed. Inner scripts we've never questioned. But this discomfort is not a flaw in the process; it *is* the process. Just as muscles ache during rehabilitation, so too does the psyche protest when we begin to feel what we've habitually bypassed. The task is not to eliminate this unease but to make room for it—to regard it as the cost of reinhabiting the self.

A further consideration is that reflection must be *protected from co-option.* In a culture of endless self-optimisation, even introspection can be warped into performance. Journaling becomes a productivity tool. Silence becomes another box to tick on a wellness list. But reflection is not about improvement in the narrow sense. It is about *integration*—gathering the fragmented parts of ourselves and sitting with what is, rather than what ought to be. It is the art of rehumanising a life that may have been colonised by metrics and momentum.

Creating internal space also requires rethinking our relationship to time. Reflection cannot be rushed. It demands spacious scheduling, not as an indulgence but as a necessity. Just as the body needs recovery between physical exertion, the psyche needs decompression between periods of stimulation. This is not a matter of time *management*, but of time *honouring.* A regular weekly window for non-doing, unstructured thought, or deep presence is not a luxury; it is psychological hygiene. Without it, we are not really choosing our lives—we are simply reacting to them.

There is also a communal dimension to this practice. While reflection is inward, it does not have to be isolated. Thoughtful dialogue with a trusted friend, therapist, or spiritual mentor can become a reflective space of its own. The key is to enter such conversations not to broadcast or impress, but to *uncover.* Reflection shared becomes reflection deepened. It grounds the private process of introspection in the public context of witness and connection.

In the end, to create internal space for reflection is to honour the self as something more than a node in a network, more than a vessel of productivity, more than a curated profile. It is to affirm that our thoughts deserve silence, that our feelings deserve attention, and that our lives deserve inquiry. It is a refusal to live only from the outside in. It is an insistence that the inner world—though invisible—is real, significant, and sacred.

And if we can reclaim that space with regularity and respect, then we begin to live not just efficiently, but *authentically*. Not just in motion, but in meaning. Not just online, but *alive*.

The Role of Sacred Journaling

There is a quiet revolution underway—one that requires no Wi-Fi, no software update, no notification settings. It begins with a pen. It deepens with attention. And it unfolds in the intimate, private space of a journal. In a world that increasingly externalises identity through performance, publication, and perpetual feedback loops, the act of writing for oneself—unguarded, uncurated, unread—has become radical. *Sacred journaling*, at its core, is not a productivity tool. It is a devotional practice. A form of personal liturgy. A mirror, not for how the world sees us, but for how we are with ourselves.

Despite being largely unmonetisable, journaling remains one of the most transformative psychological and spiritual practices available to us. It is also one of the most misunderstood. Too often dismissed as self-indulgent or adolescent, journaling is in fact a method of internal inquiry with deep roots in philosophical, religious, and therapeutic traditions. From Marcus Aurelius to Virginia Woolf, Anne Frank to James Baldwin, personal writing has served as a crucible for processing complexity, metabolising emotion, and clarifying thought. But sacred journaling goes beyond narrative or catharsis—it becomes a form of *embodied presence*. A daily detox of the mind, and a ritualised return to the self.

The modern nervous system is chronically overstimulated. It absorbs more data in a day than our ancestors encountered in a month. Emotions are suppressed for the sake of efficiency. Thoughts are fragmented by algorithmic distractions. In such an environment, unprocessed experience accumulates like psychic plaque. Journaling, then, functions as a *mental hygiene practice.* It is where thoughts are allowed to complete themselves. Where feelings are named rather than numbed. Where contradictions can coexist without the demand for premature resolution.

But the potency of sacred journaling lies not just in expression—it lies in *intention.* Sacred journaling is not a diary of daily events. Nor is it an exercise in aesthetic self-display. It is a ritualised practice of inner witnessing. You do not write for the past. You do not write for future readers. You write to come home to the now. The purpose is not to be interesting. It is to be *honest.* This is what makes the journal sacred—not because of its content, but because of the quality of consciousness it demands. The journal is the one place where we are not performing for anyone, including ourselves.

Practically speaking, the practice of sacred journaling benefits from structure—but not rigidity. Structured prompts are a powerful gateway. Questions such as *What truth am I avoiding today?*, *Where have I betrayed or honoured myself recently?*, or *What is my body asking for right now?* serve as portals to depth. They bypass the superficial recounting of events and invite the writer into their *interior weather.* Over time, such prompts train the mind to become more precise, more introspective, more attuned to nuance.

Yet there is an art to this that resists optimisation. The point is not to engineer insight, but to *make room* for it. One might write three pages without revelation, only to arrive at a single sentence that reorganises one's entire perception. This is the alchemy of sacred journaling. Clarity is not imposed. It is revealed—gently, quietly, and often when least expected.

Another layer of this practice involves reading back what has been written. Not to critique, but to *witness.* Rereading past entries offers a mirror to growth, patterns, blind spots, and forgotten wisdom. It restores a sense of narrative to what may otherwise feel chaotic or disconnected. The journal becomes not just a container for thought, but a *map of selfhood.* In times of confusion or despair, it reminds us that we have been lost before—and found our way back.

The therapeutic power of this process is well-supported. Research in narrative psychology and expressive writing has shown that journaling can reduce anxiety, enhance immune function, improve sleep, and foster post-traumatic growth. But sacred journaling does more than repair; it reveals. It brings to light the parts of ourselves that are not allowed to speak in everyday life: the grieving child, the wise elder, the fatigued soul, the ecstatic dreamer. Over time, this practice creates a more *integrated psyche.* You begin to live with less inner exile. More coherence. More peace.

Importantly, sacred journaling does not require eloquence. In fact, language that is too polished often conceals more than it reveals. Sacred journaling rewards sincerity over style, presence over polish. Grammar is irrelevant. Spelling is optional. What matters is authenticity. There is a rawness in truth that does not need to be beautiful to be powerful. A scribbled page, written in the middle of the night with a trembling hand, may hold more wisdom than an entire shelf of self-help books.

This is not to say the practice is always easy. On the contrary, sacred journaling can be profoundly uncomfortable. It may reveal truths we are not ready to accept. It may illuminate grief we thought we had buried. It may show us that the narrative we've been telling about our lives no longer holds. But this discomfort is sacred, too. It signals transformation. The journal becomes a space where we rehearse courage, name our fears, and re-choose our values. It is where healing does not require an audience.

The sacredness of the journal also lies in its *privacy*. In a culture addicted to visibility, the fact that no one else will read your words is not a limitation—it is liberation. In the absence of an audience, something astonishing happens: we tell the truth. Not the brand-safe, PR-optimised version of the truth, but the truth as it lives in the bones. The truth that trembles. The truth that liberates. In this way, journaling becomes not only reflective—it becomes redemptive.

The material tools are simple: a notebook, a pen, a quiet corner. But the inner stance matters more. Sacred journaling asks us to show up *without agenda*. Not to fix or achieve, but to *meet ourselves*. You may begin by writing about a meeting at work, and end by uncovering an unconscious fear of inadequacy. You may start by describing your morning coffee and stumble into a memory that still aches. The page holds it all without judgement. It is a sacred space precisely because it asks nothing but presence.

To build this into a daily ritual is to rewire the relationship with the self. Over time, sacred journaling becomes an anchor. A friend. A confessional. A mirror. It allows the mind to settle, the nervous system to exhale, the soul to speak. It is both a detox and a dialogue. Not because the world is toxic (though it often is), but because the psyche needs a place to *digest*. Without this digestion, experience stagnates. With it, experience becomes wisdom.

In a world where everyone is watching and everything is recorded, sacred journaling reminds us that not all truth needs to be seen to be *real*. Some truths are meant to be whispered. Some insights are meant to be earned. And some healing only happens when we stop broadcasting and begin listening—truly, deeply, courageously—to the voice within.

That voice is not always loud. But it is always there. And a blank page, held with care, is the perfect place to meet it.

Emotional Literacy in a Digitised World

We are living in the most connected age in human history—and yet, we are struggling to connect with ourselves. In an era defined by constant digital exchange, the subtle inner signals of emotion have grown faint, drowned beneath a sea of notifications, scrolling feeds, and algorithmic dopamine loops. Emotions, which once served as internal compasses, are now often mislabelled, ignored, or outsourced to external validation. As a result, many people are emotionally undernourished, experientially overfed, and psychologically adrift. The need for *emotional literacy*—the ability to name, understand, and regulate our emotions—has never been more urgent.

To be emotionally literate is not simply to be expressive or "in touch with your feelings". It is to possess the vocabulary and awareness to detect what you're experiencing, the discernment to identify its source, and the capacity to hold it without collapse or avoidance. It is a form of inner fluency. And like any language, it is learned—through attention, practice, and presence.

But in the digitised world, this learning is constantly disrupted. The platforms we inhabit are not designed for reflection; they are designed for reaction. Speed is rewarded, not nuance. Outrage is amplified, not understanding. Emotional complexity is flattened into emojis and hot takes. In this environment, a person may feel sadness but label it boredom, feel fear but express it as anger, or feel loneliness but cover it with performative productivity. The subtleties of inner life are rendered illegible when our time and attention are colonised by screens.

This distortion begins early. Children are now exposed to screens before they can walk. They are often pacified with digital devices rather than taught to sit with discomfort. Emotional regulation—once learned through attuned interpersonal connection—is now deferred to apps, animations, and algorithmic distractions. A tantrum is resolved with a tablet, a meltdown muted with media.

Over time, this conditions a profound dependency: emotional states are not to be explored, but *escaped.* The nervous system learns to outsource comfort rather than build internal resilience.

By adulthood, this disconnection becomes structural. Most adults were never taught to map their emotional states beyond crude binaries—happy, sad, angry. But the emotional spectrum is far more nuanced: frustration is not the same as disappointment; shame is distinct from guilt; anxiety is not interchangeable with fear. Without the ability to *differentiate*, emotions become a blur—and when we cannot name what we feel, we cannot *work with it.* Instead, we numb it, deny it, or project it onto others.

Social media exacerbates this emotional illiteracy in subtle ways. Curated lives breed comparison. Highlight reels create illusions of stability and success. Vulnerability is often aestheticised into performative self-disclosure, which paradoxically creates more distance than connection. The result is a quiet epidemic of emotional suppression cloaked in hyper-expression. We are louder than ever, but less understood—especially by ourselves.

To reclaim emotional literacy in this context is an act of quiet rebellion. It begins not with dramatic transformations, but with subtle, persistent questions: *What am I feeling? Where in my body do I feel it? What does it want me to know?* These are not questions the digital world will prompt you to ask—but they are the ones that build self-trust and emotional integrity.

One of the most effective tools for developing this literacy is the practice of *naming emotions accurately*. Studies in affect labelling—particularly the work of psychologist Matthew Lieberman—show that naming a feeling decreases its physiological intensity. "Name it to tame it," as the phrase goes. When we label an emotion precisely (not just "bad" but "disappointed", not just "angry" but "resentful"), the amygdala's reactivity diminishes and the prefrontal cortex becomes more engaged. In other words, the brain becomes more capable of regulation the moment we become more emotionally precise.

But precision requires space. Emotional literacy thrives not in rush, but in reflection. Silence becomes a necessary precondition. Disconnection from devices becomes essential—not as rejection of technology, but as *reclamation of attention.* Without quiet, emotion cannot surface clearly. Without slowness, we cannot hear what the body is trying to say.

Another often-overlooked dimension of emotional literacy is *permission.* Many people struggle to name their emotions not because they lack vocabulary, but because they do not feel they are *allowed* to feel what they feel. Cultural conditioning plays a major role here: men may be discouraged from expressing sadness, women from expressing anger, leaders from expressing uncertainty. Emotional suppression, in this context, is not just a personal habit—it is a socially reinforced expectation.

Healing this requires not only self-awareness but *self-compassion.* Emotional literacy without compassion can easily become another form of inner policing—a tendency to pathologise or overanalyse every feeling. But the goal is not to "fix" your emotions. It is to *listen to them.* Emotions are not problems to be solved; they are messages to be understood. Each emotion contains information. Fear may be pointing to a boundary. Sadness may be asking for rest. Anger may be a call to reclaim agency. When we relate to emotions as signals, not enemies, they begin to guide rather than overwhelm us.

Moreover, developing emotional literacy in a digitised world requires reclaiming *embodiment.* Emotions are not just cognitive—they are *somatic.* A clenched jaw, a tight chest, a hollow stomach: these are not separate from our emotional life; they *are* our emotional life, expressed in the body. When we tune into physical sensations, we bypass the noisy mind and reconnect to felt experience. Practices such as somatic tracking, body scans, and breathwork re-anchor attention in the body and create space for emotional integration without verbal overload.

But emotional literacy is not merely an individual endeavour. It has collective stakes. In a society where emotional repression is normalised and empathy is scarce, cultivating emotional literacy becomes a civic responsibility. It allows us to relate to one another not as caricatures, but as complex human beings. It enables dialogue rather than division, connection rather than reaction. In this way, emotional literacy is a cultural medicine. One that invites nuance, depth, and humanity back into our relational field.

Practical tools can support this. Emotion wheels help build nuanced vocabulary. Journaling prompts foster reflective engagement. Psychotherapy offers guided exploration. Mindful conversations—where we speak from emotion rather than narrative—restore authenticity in relationships. But tools are only as effective as the *presence* we bring to them. The essence of emotional literacy is not technique—it is *attunement.*

We must become willing to feel what we feel before we try to "understand" it. We must resist the digital demand to be "fine" and choose, instead, to be *real.* This may mean pausing before replying to a message. Taking a breath before responding to a trigger. Saying "I don't know what I'm feeling yet" instead of faking certainty. These are small acts—but they reclaim emotional sovereignty. They rebuild trust in our internal compass.

Ultimately, emotional literacy in a digitised world is about remembering that the quality of our inner life matters. That our emotions are not distractions from intelligence—they *are* intelligence. That the point of being connected to everyone else is meaningless if we are disconnected from ourselves. And that in a world saturated with noise, the quiet truth of what we're feeling may be the most important signal of all.

The Return of Intuition

In a culture that fetishises data, logic, and external metrics of success, intuition has become an endangered faculty. It is often relegated to the realm of mysticism or dismissed as unreliable in favour of what can be quantified and optimised. And yet, some of the most critical decisions in life—whom to trust, when to leave, what truly matters—cannot be answered by spreadsheets, algorithms, or second-hand advice. They require something deeper, older, and more embodied: a felt sense of knowing that arises not from reasoning, but from resonance. That faculty is intuition. And we are, increasingly, losing access to it.

The reason is not simply cultural—it is neurological. Intuition arises from a brain-body dialogue that is easily drowned out by overstimulation. In the age of digital excess, the human nervous system is perpetually in response mode. Notifications, alerts, headlines, and hyperlinked distractions keep the mind fragmented and the body reactive. The result is an attentional landscape that is outwardly scattered and inwardly muted. We are constantly fed *input*, but seldom given time or stillness to digest it. Intuition, by contrast, requires precisely what the digital world disrupts: internal spaciousness, bodily awareness, and the ability to *feel* into what is not yet fully formed.

To understand how overstimulation silences intuition, we must first recognise where intuition lives—not in the intellect, but in the body. The vagus nerve, often referred to as the body's information superhighway, is a central channel in the gut-brain axis. It carries data not only from the brain to the body, but from the body to the brain—especially from the gut. Research shows that the enteric nervous system (the "second brain" in the gastrointestinal tract) plays a key role in mood regulation and decision-making. This is why we speak of having a "gut feeling." That language is not metaphorical; it is neurobiological. But when the body is dysregulated—constantly tense, fatigued, or dissociated—those subtle signals never make it to conscious awareness. They are intercepted by adrenaline, numbed by cortisol, or overwritten by dopamine-driven distraction.

In this context, it is no surprise that many people report feeling chronically unsure of themselves. Not because they lack intelligence or information, but because their inner compass has been distorted. We are encouraged to Google before we reflect, to consult devices before tuning inward. This constant outsourcing erodes the muscle of self-trust. Over time, we forget how to feel what we feel, let alone follow it. Decision fatigue, existential confusion, and emotional numbness become not personal failings, but symptoms of a disembodied culture.

Reclaiming intuition, then, is not about developing a new skill—it is about *remembering* an old one. It is about peeling back the noise to hear what has always been there: the body's quiet guidance. This does not mean rejecting reason or logic. Intuition is not anti-rational. It is *pre*-rational. It arises before the analytical mind has taken over—not in opposition to it, but alongside it. The healthiest decision-making integrates both: the brain's analysis and the body's knowing. But in a society obsessed with metrics and mental performance, we must consciously re-centre the role of inner sensing.

So how does one listen again?

First, by slowing down. Intuition is not loud. It does not compete for attention the way an app notification does. It whispers. And like any whisper, it can only be heard when the external volume is lowered. This is why intuition tends to emerge in moments of solitude, rest, or sensory quietude—on a walk without a phone, during meditation, after a good night's sleep. The more overstimulated the system, the less accessible intuitive insight becomes. Stillness is not optional; it is *required.*

Second, by grounding back into the body. Intuition is a *felt* sense. You cannot think your way into it. Practices that restore somatic awareness—such as breathwork, body scans, and conscious movement—create the conditions for that felt sense to surface. The key is not to analyse what arises, but to *stay with it.* A sensation in the chest, a tightening in the stomach, a pulling toward or away from a person or situation—these are the breadcrumbs of intuition. We must learn to notice without immediately translating them into words. This somatic patience is a discipline. It is also a gateway.

Third, by discerning between fear and knowing. This is perhaps the most common obstacle. Both fear and intuition can manifest as caution, but their *texture* is different. Fear is noisy, frantic, urgent. Intuition is calm, grounded, and quietly insistent. Fear screams. Intuition nudges. Learning to distinguish the two takes practice, but a useful heuristic is this: if the impulse is coming from contraction (urgency, scarcity, panic), it's likely fear. If it arises from clarity and stillness, even if it's uncomfortable, it is more likely intuition.

Another important practice is creating regular intervals for *check-in.* Most people only consult their intuition in times of crisis. But intuition, like any language, becomes clearer with frequent dialogue. Daily journaling, silent pauses before decisions, and rituals of inquiry (such as "What does my body say?") build this fluency over time. The goal is not to force answers, but to remain available to them.

It is also helpful to acknowledge that intuition is not always immediate or neat. Sometimes it arrives as a subtle dissonance—a vague sense that something is off, even if you can't yet explain why. Sometimes it speaks through dreams, synchronicities, or repeated patterns in conversation. The point is to *stay open*, even when the rational mind is impatient. Clarity often arrives indirectly. Intuition rewards those who wait with attentiveness, not those who rush with certainty.

This process of reconnection is not merely a psychological adjustment. It is a philosophical reorientation. It challenges the mechanistic worldview that treats the body as a machine and the mind as its operator. It calls us to remember that intelligence is not confined to the skull. It lives in the tissues, the nervous system, the viscera. It pulses through sensation and image, not just thought. When we honour this, we do not become less rational—we become more *whole.*

And in a world that fragments our attention, fractures our presence, and flattens our inner life into click-throughs and algorithms, wholeness is radical. Intuition is not an indulgence. It is a reclamation. A return to something primal, and profoundly sane.

Because sometimes, the wisest part of you is not the one with the clever argument or the polished plan. It's the part that just *knows.* The part that feels something is right before the facts can confirm it. The part that says no, quietly but firmly, even when the world is saying yes.

To live by that part is not to abandon thinking. It is to let the deepest parts of you *vote.* Not the loudest, not the most socially reinforced—but the truest. And in an age of hyper-rational overwhelm, that may be the most intelligent choice of all.

Building a Ritual of Self-Check-In

There is a quiet tragedy unfolding beneath the speed of modern life. While the world has never been louder—more connected, more surveilled, more documented—it has also never been more internally estranged. The tools we use to stay in touch with the world have made it easier to lose touch with ourselves. We swipe through updates but forget to check in with the one person most in need of attention: the one behind the screen. This is not a sentimental observation—it is a psychological, physiological, and existential imperative. In a culture of external metrics and digital noise, we must learn to develop practices of inner attunement. Not occasionally. *Ritually.*

The concept of a "soul weather report" may sound quaint in the age of neuro-optimisation and biohacking dashboards, but its roots are ancient and its relevance urgent. This is not about introspection for its own sake. It is about cultivating the ability to locate oneself in one's emotional, mental, and spiritual landscape with the same accuracy we expect from GPS in physical space. If you don't know where you are internally, you can't choose your next right step. You're not living—you're reacting.

The ritual of self-check-in is not a therapeutic technique. It is a life skill. And like any skill, it requires a rhythm, a framework, and a sense of sacred regularity.

At its core, a self-check-in ritual is a deliberate pause to ask one deceptively simple question: *What is true right now?* Not what should be true. Not what you wish were true. But what is actually, *unmistakably* alive within you. And then, without fixing, fleeing, or judging the answer—you stay. You listen. You witness.

But to truly make this a practice—rather than a passing idea—structure helps. The most resilient check-in rituals are the ones that are repeatable, personal, and sensorially grounded.

Begin with *when.* Morning and evening are natural portals—thresholds between states of being. A brief morning check-in sets the compass before the world intrudes. An evening check-in acts as a digestif, helping the psyche metabolise the day. But the point is not when you do it—it's *that* you do it. Anchor it to an existing habit if needed: after brushing your teeth, before your first sip of coffee, or as the final act before bed.

Then choose *how.* Some may prefer silent reflection. Others may need the ritualising presence of pen and paper. Journaling, done with intention, becomes not a performance but a mirror. Prompts like "What feels heavy right now?" or "Where is ease showing up?" help bypass surface chatter and sink into deeper awareness. For those more somatically inclined, a body scan can be revelatory—observing where tension collects, where breath is restricted, or where warmth resides. The body often knows before the mind does.

Others may benefit from visualisation: imagining themselves as a weather system and describing the internal climate—stormy, humid, overcast, radiant. This poetic framing helps decouple identity from mood. You are not the storm. You are the sky it passes through.

The most profound check-ins include three levels of inquiry:

Emotional – What am I feeling right now? Not just "good" or "bad," but specific granularity. Irritated? Grateful? Uncertain? Numb? Naming emotions builds emotional literacy, and what we name we can tend.

Cognitive – What stories am I telling myself today? What thought patterns are looping? Are they true? Are they useful?

Somatic – What is happening in my body? Tight jaw? Shallow breath? Restlessness? The body keeps score—and it also tells the truth.

Bringing these threads together is not a performance. You're not trying to produce insight. You're practising *relationship*. The goal is to become a better host to your inner world. To turn toward your experience, however it shows up, with the steadiness of someone who refuses to abandon themselves.

This is not always comfortable. Sometimes what arises in these moments is resistance. Boredom. Guilt. The urge to reach for a device, a distraction, an escape hatch. That too is information. The compulsion to exit the self is a signal that something vital is being bypassed. Staying with discomfort—curiously, kindly—is itself a revolution in a culture of avoidance.

Over time, these rituals shift one's baseline. The person who checks in daily becomes less reactive, more self-aware, and—most importantly—more internally trustworthy. They begin to live from response, not reactivity. From clarity, not confusion.

It's also worth noting that self-check-in is not the same as self-analysis. Analysis dissects. Check-in *notices*. There is no agenda other than presence. In a world obsessed with fixing, improving, and "leveling up," this return to observation without evaluation is radical. It says: I am worth witnessing as I am—not only when I am optimised.

This ritual becomes especially potent when extended to moments of decision-making, relational friction, or overwhelm. Pausing to ask, "What is happening *in me* right now?" often reveals far more than reacting on autopilot ever could. It creates a pocket of sovereignty in the chaos. A space to choose, not just cope.

Over time, this becomes an act of spiritual hygiene—on par with brushing teeth or washing hands. Just as we cleanse the body, we must also clear the inner clutter. The sediment of unprocessed emotion, unacknowledged fear, or joy left uncelebrated does not disappear—it festers. A self-check-in clears the channel.

And as the practice deepens, something profound occurs. The act of checking in stops being a task and becomes a form of intimacy. A rendezvous with the self. A reaffirmation that you are not just a vessel of productivity, not merely a user interface for external approval, but a living, sensing, sovereign being worthy of your own attention.

This is not soft. This is foundational. In a world that monetises your distraction and profits from your disconnection, the choice to self-attune is nothing short of defiant. It is how you remember what it feels like to be *you*—not your performance, not your persona, but the quiet, living pulse beneath it all.

And perhaps that is the most radical act of all: to refuse to be a stranger to your own inner life.

To pause.

To ask.

To listen.

To stay.

Chapter 8
Digital Spaces, Sacred Boundaries

We shape the environments we inhabit—and in return, they mould us. Churchill once made this observation about architecture, but today, its resonance is startlingly more acute in the realm of digital architecture. We live within invisible infrastructures, drift through algorithmically curated timelines, and clutch in our hands devices that dissolve the boundary between what is ours and what's been quietly fed to us. These are not abstract shifts; they are etched into our bodies. We feel them in the exhaustion that never quite lifts, the attention that splinters, the constant hum of a nervous system unable to stand down. In such a climate, setting boundaries isn't simply an exercise in discipline—it's an affirmation of dignity.

This chapter isn't a pitch for digital minimalism dressed up in sleek aesthetics. It doesn't ask you to tidy up your apps or colour-code your calendar. Rather, it suggests that creating boundaries is, at its core, a spiritual undertaking. Without gates, everything enters. And when everything enters, the self becomes porous—no longer able to distinguish between what arises from within and what has been seeded from without. Sacred boundaries, then, are how we begin to draw a line—not to exclude the world, but to find ourselves again within it.

Time, unsurprisingly, is the first arena in which this reclamation must unfold. And more specifically, those liminal moments at the bookends of each day: the first and last thirty minutes. These may seem like inconsequential margins. They are anything but. Morning and night are thresholds, quiet gates through which the nervous system calibrates itself. Reaching for a phone before the mind has even fully returned to the body is not a harmless reflex—it's a disorientation. It gives the external world the first word. Ending the day bathed in blue light is no less costly; it interrupts the descent into rest that evening was meant to offer. This chapter doesn't come wielding shame or ascetic guilt. Instead, it extends an invitation. Not to 'detox' in the trendy, fleeting sense—but to rewire your patterns.

A device-free dawn and dusk isn't a performance; it's a profound gesture of self-authorship.

Of course, time alone does not hold the boundary. Space matters too. Environments speak, even when we don't listen. When every room becomes digitally accessible, when every surface glows with the potential for work or distraction, the body is nowhere fully present. What was once home becomes, subtly but unmistakably, a battleground: between attention and attrition, rest and relentless reach. This chapter turns to the practical: how we might reimagine our domestic spaces as tech-free sanctuaries—not nostalgic retreats, but thoughtful choices. A bedroom that fosters sleep. A kitchen that fosters presence. A living room where books, instruments, and shared silences aren't relics but living practices. These aren't arbitrary exclusions. They are rituals—acts of care, of clarity, of remembering what the space is for.

But if structure becomes hollow performance, it's soon abandoned. Which is why we next move into the idea of a digital diet—not as abstinence, but as curation. This isn't about renunciation for its own sake. It's about asking different questions. The same way we've learnt to distinguish between food that fills us and food that nourishes, we must begin to reckon with our informational intake. What are we consuming, and why? Does it enrich, or does it deplete? This isn't a puritan's call to purity—it's a call to consciousness. Algorithms feed on indiscriminate craving. Meaning, on the other hand, is selective. It requires choice.

And choice, inevitably, requires saying no. Not aggressively. Not apologetically either. Boundaries have long been misunderstood as harsh or unkind. But that is a distortion. A boundary is not a barricade. It is a container—a space within which something precious can thrive. Saying no can, in fact, be an act of generosity, when done with clarity and respect. This chapter doesn't stop at theory. It offers language. Scripts and phrases that help you turn down the invitations that dislocate you from your rhythm—be they digital demands or social obligations. Because every yes uttered from guilt or habit is a quiet theft from what actually matters.

At the heart of it all, sacred boundaries are not about escape. They are about creating a foundation from which one can truly engage. The goal is not to reject the digital world outright, but to stop sleepwalking through it. To interrupt the auto-pilot. To live in a way that doesn't require constant escape, because the life itself has been shaped—deliberately—to support presence, clarity, and coherence.

This is no nostalgic yearning for some pre-digital Eden. It is a coming of age. A passage from passive participation to deliberate design. To establish a boundary in an attention economy is, make no mistake, a radical act. To guard your silence in a world that peddles noise is a form of protest. And in an age where connection is often confused with contact, the spaces we preserve become sacred—places where something real might emerge.

What you'll find in the pages that follow is not a manifesto, nor a list of commandments. It is a kind of map—a set of practices rooted in neuroscience, psychological insight, and lived experience. It's an offering to help you become, once again, the steward of your own mental landscape. The premise is simple, though hardly easy: sovereignty in the digital age begins with boundary-making in the physical one. And that boundary, far from a line of exclusion, is a bridge—back to presence, back to meaning, and ultimately, back to yourself.

Reclaiming the First and Last 30 Minutes of Your Day

Why a device-free start and finish rewires your nervous system, restores sovereignty, and reframes time as sacred.

We do not merely *check our phones*—we outsource our sense of self to them. Every morning swipe and nightly scroll acts as a nervous system contract: an unconscious agreement to let the external world dictate our inner tempo. Few habits have more quietly shaped the modern psyche than this digital trespass into our most neurologically plastic, psychologically impressionable windows of time—the first and last 30 minutes of each day.

To understand the cost of surrendering these margins of consciousness to screens, we must begin not with productivity hacks or sleep studies, but with the biology of attention and the existential posture of awakening.

The first moments of waking are not neutral—they are neurologically sacred. Upon rising, the brain transitions from deep sleep into theta waves—a state that is both malleable and meditative, where suggestibility is high and habitual patterns consolidate quickly. To place a screen—filled with novelty, urgency, and external stimulus—in front of this tender neurological soil is to plant chaos in our mental garden before we've even stretched. And at night, as we attempt to descend from the overstimulated peaks of the day, the blue-lit glow of our devices denies our physiology the cues it needs to soften. We do not land into rest—we crash.

What's at stake in reclaiming these bookends is not just better sleep or improved focus. It is our capacity for sovereignty. By choosing to begin and end our days without digital interference, we signal to the body: *I am home in myself. I am not a reaction. I am a rhythm.* The effects are subtle but cumulative, like daily tuning a string instrument. We recalibrate not just what we pay attention to, but *how* we attend.

This shift is not about purism. It is not moralistic. It is about reorienting toward rhythm instead of reactivity. When the first thing we touch in the morning is a glass of water instead of a glass screen, the body responds in kind. When the final minutes before sleep are devoted to reflection, breathing, or stillness—rather than replies, likes, and endless tabs—we do not just *sleep better*, we *process differently.* Our dreams deepen. Our insights ripen. We recover space in the architecture of the self that has been colonised by urgency.

Contemporary neuroscience underscores the importance of these transitions. The brain's default mode network—linked to memory consolidation, creativity, and self-awareness—is activated during moments of quiet and inward attention. But when these moments are interrupted by stimulus—especially from social media or news—

we hijack the very networks that give us insight. Instead of integration, we ingest. Instead of renewal, we rehearse stress.

Yet cultural norms continue to treat device dependency in these windows as benign. Waking up to email is seen as diligence. Falling asleep with YouTube in hand is common. But what appears mundane is metabolically monumental. Cortisol spikes. Melatonin is suppressed. Dopaminergic systems are prematurely hijacked, creating the neurochemical equivalent of starting the day with dessert and ending it with an argument.

A growing body of research reveals the psychological cost: diminished emotional regulation, shorter attention spans, and an increased baseline of anxiety. But beyond the data lies the deeper loss—*the erosion of ritual.*

Ritual is what distinguishes transition from transaction. The first and last thirty minutes of your day are, at their core, rituals of becoming. They frame your relationship to time, self, and the sacred. The digital world thrives on interruption and immediacy. The human nervous system thrives on rhythm and reverence.

To reclaim these liminal thresholds, then, is to make a quiet political act—a rebellion not through resistance, but through refusal. A refusal to allow the most impressionable moments of our day to be dictated by code we didn't write, by agendas we didn't choose, by algorithms that do not honour our wholeness.

In the next section, we'll explore practical strategies and meaningful alternatives that go beyond the typical "turn off notifications" advice. Because this is not about discipline. It's about dignity.

The challenge with digital habits is not that they are inherently harmful—it's that they are *default.* And defaults become destiny when left unexamined. Most of us did not choose to begin and end our days staring into handheld portals. We simply slipped into it, seduced by convenience and anchored by social norms that value accessibility over autonomy. But the same mechanism that allowed this slide—habit—can be reversed through ritual.

So, what does it look like to rehumanise these margins of the day?

It begins not with restriction, but with replacement. The nervous system doesn't respond well to deprivation. It craves rhythm, meaning, and sensory grounding. Simply removing the phone is insufficient. We must *replace the noise with signal.*

Morning as a Return, Not a Race

Instead of grabbing your phone upon waking, consider placing a tactile object at your bedside—a book, a journal, a smooth stone. Something real. Something weighty. Let the first act of the day involve touch, breath, and presence.

Engage with something that connects you to *you* before the world arrives. This could mean five minutes of breath awareness. It could be a simple journal prompt: *What do I need today?* It could be stretching with closed eyes, orienting yourself not to news but to body. It's not about productivity. It's about presence.

Neurologically, this matters. Those first thirty minutes are when your brain is shifting from delta to theta to alpha waves. It is a time when inputs become imprints. What you consume during this window enters the psyche unfiltered—like dye in water. This is not a time for urgency. It's a time for calibration.

Evening as a Descent, Not a Dump

The same applies to night. Most people use digital devices in bed as a way to *decompress*. But what they are actually doing is *deferring processing*. Blue light aside, what disturbs our sleep is not the screen itself—it's the stories, the stimulation, and the unfinished loops it creates.

To unwind effectively is to *allow digestion*—of thoughts, of feelings, of experience. Create a buffer zone of at least thirty minutes between your last screen interaction and sleep. Replace it with a ritual of descent: light stretching, scent, reflection, or stillness. This is not about self-improvement—it's about self-integration.

The research here is clear: people who avoid screens in the hour before bed fall asleep faster, experience deeper REM sleep, and report higher morning clarity. But more than that, they enter sleep *as themselves*, not as a digital echo.

Crafting a New Cultural Norm

Reclaiming the bookends of your day is not just a personal wellness strategy. It's a cultural intervention. In a society that confuses availability with value, choosing to be *unavailable*—even for 30 minutes—is a radical reassertion of selfhood.

It says: I choose internal clarity over external commentary. I prioritise coherence over consumption. I am not a vessel for urgency—I am a vessel for rhythm.

This reframing also offers a corrective to the toxic myths of modern hustle culture. You are not behind because you didn't check email before coffee. You are not indulgent because you closed the laptop at sunset. You are not failing because your phone spent the night in another room.

You are healing.

You are remembering that before you are a consumer of information, you are a body. A being. A presence. And the nervous system does not speak the language of speed. It speaks the language of sequence, repetition, and pause.

Begin Again, Twice a Day

This is the quiet power of reclaiming the first and last 30 minutes. Twice each day, you get to begin again—not in reaction to noise, but in relation to self. This is not just a behavioural change. It's a spiritual repositioning. One that restores your attention as a sacred resource. One that makes time not something to fill, but something to honour.

The practice is simple. The effects are profound.

Don't just start your day. *Arrive in it.*

Don't just end your day. *Descend into it.*

And in doing so, discover what it means to belong to yourself again—at the margins of the world, where true sovereignty begins.

Creating a Sanctuary Within Your Home

There is an irony at the heart of the digital age: we are more connected than ever, and yet the spaces we inhabit—homes, offices, even our own minds—have never felt more invaded. The average person checks their phone within ten minutes of waking and falls asleep to the hum of a screen. With boundaries dissolved by endless notifications, spatial sanctity has quietly eroded. In its place: a low-grade hum of tension, a nervous system in a constant state of readiness, and an attention span thinned to the point of fray. What was once a haven for rest and renewal now serves as a relay station for other people's demands. And so the need to reclaim home as sanctuary has become less an aesthetic preference and more a psychological imperative.

This is not an abstract concern—it is a biological one. Environments shape internal states. The spatial field in which we live either scaffolds our sense of presence or fractures it. The brain, ever plastic, mirrors its surroundings. When we habitually work from the same bed we sleep in, or scroll through emails at the dinner table, the boundaries between activity and rest blur. This ambiguity breeds chronic overstimulation, and in turn, emotional exhaustion. It is no longer enough to seek balance—we must design for it.

Creating a sanctuary within your home does not require square footage or elaborate interiors. It demands intention. It begins by recognising that the spaces we move through are not neutral—they carry psychological weight. A cluttered room breeds mental agitation. A chaotic entryway becomes an energetic bottleneck. Conversely, a clean, sunlit corner reserved for morning tea can serve as a daily touchstone for calm. The goal is not minimalism for its own sake, but resonance: cultivating areas that support nervous system regulation, emotional clarity, and soul-level restoration.

One of the most powerful interventions is the creation of tech-free zones. These are not punitive restrictions but invitations—an architectural expression of value. The bedroom, for instance, is an ideal candidate. Sleep hygiene research repeatedly confirms that the presence of phones, tablets, or TVs in the sleeping space disrupts circadian rhythms, compromises melatonin production, and fragments the brain's transition into deep rest. Reclaiming the bedroom as a sacred space—devoid of digital intrusion—can recalibrate not just sleep quality but waking vitality.

But boundaries must go beyond the bedroom. Consider the dining table. Historically a site of nourishment, dialogue, and relational intimacy, it has become in many homes a secondary desk or passive consumption hub. By consciously removing devices during meals—not just physically, but psychologically—we restore the act of eating to its rightful place: an embodied, relational ritual. The same applies to entryways. What do you encounter the moment you step inside? Is it a pile of mail, a glaring television, or the soft presence of light and stillness? Small adjustments to these transition zones create a sense of arrival—both physically and emotionally.

A sanctuary is not a retreat from the world but a reinforcement of what matters most. It signals to the psyche: here, you can exhale. Here, you are not required to perform, reply, impress, or compare. Here, you are invited to return to yourself.

The effort to cultivate tech-free zones is not merely about removing distractions; it is a gesture of reclamation—of space, of time, and ultimately, of attention. In an economy that monetises our gaze, preserving a zone where one's attention cannot be purchased becomes an act of quiet rebellion. But it is also an act of nourishment. The nervous system is not designed for continuous partial attention. It is designed for rhythm—for alternation between engagement and restoration, for moments of presence unmediated by alerts or feeds. Spatial boundaries become the container for that rhythm.

Importantly, creating a sanctuary does not require perfection. It requires ritual. A single chair by a window, reserved for reading or breathing, becomes over time a neurological anchor. Each return reinforces the association: this is where I settle. A low shelf for meaningful objects—a journal, a candle, a stone from a recent walk—can turn an ordinary corner into a sacred nook. The key is consistency and intention. When certain physical locations are repeatedly paired with presence, rest, or reflection, the brain begins to anticipate and mirror those internal states the moment you enter them. This is not decoration; this is environmental entrainment.

There is also a broader cultural tension at play. The prevailing ethos prizes utility. Every space, like every hour, must justify itself through output. A room that exists solely for silence or contemplation is often viewed as indulgent. But this mindset is itself part of the digital pathology: the commodification of every square inch, every waking moment. Sanctuary defies that logic. It does not exist to optimise, but to restore. In a home governed by this ethic, not everything needs to be monetised, streamed, stored, or shared. Some spaces exist simply for being.

This shift is not without friction. If you live with others—partners, children, flatmates—the creation of sanctuary requires conversation, not imposition. It requires shared agreements about where and how technology enters communal spaces. For families, this might mean a charging station in the hallway, where devices are parked during meals or before bed. For cohabiting adults, it might mean co-designing a screen-free Sunday morning or a no-phones zone in the living room. These boundaries do not restrict freedom; they reframe it. They help clarify the subtle difference between convenience and connection, between access and intimacy.

In a culture that insists we remain always on, a home that allows you to be off is radical. But radical in the old sense of the word: from the root. It returns us to something essential. It reminds us that the quality of our days is shaped not only by what we do, but by where we are invited to stop doing.

Designing such sanctuaries also invites us to reassess the sensory palette of our homes. Much of the digital environment is dominated by high-frequency stimulation—blue light, abrupt notifications, flickering video. Sanctuary space calls for the opposite: warm light, natural textures, acoustic softness. A shift from digital glare to organic calm. Curtains that diffuse sunlight instead of LED strips that mimic it. A small indoor plant that invites slowness rather than another screen to fill the field of vision. Even scent becomes a cue—lavender, cedar, frankincense—each one grounding the body in now, reawakening our olfactory memory, which, unlike screens, never lies.

It is worth noting that sanctuary need not be static. The idea is not to create a room that excludes life, but a zone that includes the self. A sanctuary might be mobile—a bag that always contains a journal, a thermos, a novel. It might be temporary—a ritual of laying out a mat and lighting a candle before bed. The essential element is not permanence, but intention. The act of choosing presence over passivity, of preparing the mind to inhabit the body fully. In this way, sanctuary is as much about practice as place.

This reframing becomes especially vital when we consider how digital spaces have collapsed boundaries. Work enters the bedroom. News enters the kitchen. Everyone else's life enters our quietest hour. Creating sanctuary is not just spatial hygiene—it is psychic repair. It is how we remember that not all inputs are equal, and not all hours should be mined for output.

There's a paradox at the heart of sanctuary: the more we honour it, the less we need to escape from our own lives. A home with sanctuary woven into its daily architecture becomes a dwelling that doesn't just house us but holds us. It becomes a place not just of sleep, storage, and streaming—but of return. Return to breath. Return to slowness. Return to self.

In the end, the question is not whether we can make space for sanctuary. It is whether we can afford not to. The nervous system does not operate on Wi-Fi. It calibrates to rhythm, safety, silence, and presence. A sanctuary is where that calibration becomes possible again—not because we've disconnected, but because we've remembered what we were connected to in the first place.

This is not interior design. This is inner alignment.

Conscious Curation of Your Digital Diet

It is no longer enough to merely speak of "digital detox." The phrase evokes deprivation, a corrective punishment for our screen-saturated sins. But what if the real invitation is not abstinence, but discernment? In a culture that gorges on content and then collapses under the weight of its own distraction, we are called to do something far more radical than unplug—we are called to curate. Not just what we consume online, but why we consume it, how it shapes us, and whether it aligns with the life we claim to value.

The idea of a "digital diet" has become trendy in recent years, often framed with the urgency of a crash cleanse: delete the apps, silence the notifications, escape the noise. But like all quick fixes, these gestures rarely address the root issue. Because beneath our digital habits lies something deeper than lack of discipline—there is a crisis of meaning. We scroll not merely to be informed or entertained, but to feel tethered, seen, soothed, or simply to escape our inner landscape. Digital consumption is emotional consumption. And until we understand this, our relationship with the online world will remain reactive, compulsive, and malnourishing.

To curate a digital diet is to reclaim authorship over your attention. It is to become not a passive consumer, but a conscious editor of your own mental environment. And like all editorial choices, this one demands clarity of intention. The question is not only, "What am I watching or reading?" but "What kind of self is this input cultivating?" Are we reinforcing values of fear, comparison, outrage, and distraction? Or are we nurturing curiosity, depth, and joy?

The stakes are not small. Studies in cognitive psychology and neuroscience show that repeated exposure to fragmented, emotionally charged media reshapes neural pathways, fostering hyper-vigilance, emotional fatigue, and shortened attention spans. A 2023 study from the University of Pennsylvania found that people who intentionally limited their news and social media input to specific, purpose-driven windows reported not only lower stress but greater clarity in decision-making and interpersonal interactions. Their brains were not just quieter—they were more coherent.

But clarity is not achieved by abstinence alone. It is achieved by selection. A conscious digital diet begins with treating content the way one might treat food—not all calories are equal, and neither are clicks. Junk information may fill us quickly but leaves us depleted. Just as a diet of processed sugar can dull the palate, so too can a feed of hyperbole and spectacle blunt our inner compass. In contrast, intellectually nutritious content—books, podcasts, essays, long-form interviews—stimulates deeper thought and invites reflection rather than reaction. It slows us down enough to notice what matters.

Yet the curation of meaning requires more than swapping bad inputs for good ones. It demands a values-based architecture: a personal framework that helps us filter the infinite stream through a finite set of criteria. What do I want to feel more of in my life—peace, curiosity, connection, awe? Then what kinds of digital spaces, creators, and conversations actually foster those states?

This values-based curation turns the digital environment from a liability into a tool. It allows technology to serve your life, rather than shape your identity by default. For example, if your intention is to nurture curiosity, you may find more sustenance in a long-form conversation between scientists or thinkers than in a barrage of hot takes. If your intention is to cultivate calm, you might follow creators who share meditative soundscapes, contemplative essays, or simple visual poetry rather than those who trade in urgency and alarm. *It is not about avoiding stimulation—it is about choosing the right kind.*

An equally vital layer of digital curation is rhythm. Not just what you consume, but *when* and *how often*. Just as the human digestive system benefits from rest between meals, the mind requires cognitive pauses. The constant influx of information, even when it's positive or educational, creates decision fatigue and dulls emotional nuance. The design of our digital environment rarely supports mental spaciousness, so we must create it ourselves. This might mean structured blocks of online engagement, sacred device-free mornings and evenings, or an intentional weekly pause from content altogether.

Curation also implies deletion—not only of apps and accounts, but of assumed obligations. The pressure to "stay informed," to "be responsive," to "keep up with everything"—these are not moral imperatives. They are marketing narratives. You are not a bad citizen if you step away from the news for a weekend. You are not a bad friend if you don't comment on every story. You are not a failure if you decide that some forms of digital life simply do not align with who you are becoming. These small permissions are not signs of withdrawal; they are acts of sovereignty.

Importantly, conscious digital curation is not about creating an echo chamber. It is not the avoidance of difference but the cultivation of coherence. To hear opposing views is vital for empathy and growth.

But that too must be curated—sought out through credible sources and long-form discourse, not delivered through baiting algorithms that confuse provocation with relevance. *Healthy disagreement nourishes. Manufactured outrage drains.*

As you begin to shift your digital diet, you may notice something subtle and profound: a return of emotional clarity. Without the constant noise of ambient anxiety, your inner voice becomes more audible. Without the compulsive pull of comparison, your own desires begin to re-emerge. This clarity is not accidental—it is the result of mental ecology. Like a forest cleared of invasive species, your inner landscape begins to breathe again.

But this clarity requires maintenance. Algorithms, like weeds, return quickly. That's why the most effective digital diets are not "detoxes" but rituals. Just as one might tend to a garden weekly, conscious curation must become a regular practice—reviewing your inputs, noticing your emotional responses, pruning what no longer serves, and inviting in what nourishes. Over time, these small acts create not only better days but a more intentional life.

What we consume, digitally or otherwise, becomes part of us. It colours our language, fuels our moods, and sculpts our attention. Therefore, curating our digital intake is not a luxury for the hyper-organised—it is a foundational practice for anyone who values agency over their mental and emotional wellbeing.

To reinforce this practice, it can be useful to formalise your intentions. Create a set of personal principles for your digital engagement. These might include constraints ("No scrolling before breakfast" or "No news after 8 p.m."), values ("I follow accounts that teach, not preach"), or rituals ("I read one long-form piece every Sunday morning with tea"). These are not rules to rigidly obey but scaffolds that protect your cognitive clarity and emotional spaciousness.

Moreover, consider the architectural dimension of your digital life. Just as you wouldn't leave every window in your home open at all times, not every app or platform deserves constant access to your nervous system. Use technology's built-in settings—mute notifications, unfollow liberally, disable autoplay. These tweaks are not trivial. They are boundary-setting tools. Think of them as digital feng shui: design your information environment to support peace, focus, and meaning.

You might also reframe your device itself. Rather than a portal for constant stimulation, let it become a vessel for intentional presence. A smartphone can be a library, a notepad, a creative studio, a breathwork guide, a sacred archive of photographs. But only if you use it that way. When technology is deliberately repurposed from reactive to reflective, the digital becomes a conduit for consciousness—not a trap for attention.

Crucially, this process is not about perfection. There will be days when you scroll aimlessly or binge on banality. That's human. The point is not to shame these moments but to notice them—to reflect on how they feel, what they cost, and whether they align with the kind of life you're crafting. *Conscious curation is not a performance. It is a practice.* Like any practice, it deepens with repetition, gentleness, and honesty.

Ultimately, a curated digital life is not smaller or more restricted. It is richer. It creates room for nuance, for reflection, for deep reading and slow thinking. It makes space for real conversations, quiet mornings, unhurried meals, and sleep that actually restores. It brings the body back into the room, the heart back into the mind, and the self back into its rightful place—not as a passive consumer, but as a discerning author of experience.

In a world built on algorithms optimised for addiction, choosing what to consume becomes a radical act. Curating your digital diet is not simply a lifestyle adjustment—it is a philosophical stance. It says:

My mind is not a marketplace. My time is not a commodity. My attention is not for sale.

And from that stance, a new kind of freedom begins.

The Art of Saying No to Noise

It begins with a phantom itch—the compulsion to check. Your phone buzzes, or maybe it doesn't, but your attention fractures anyway. In that instant, your inner world yields to something external, ambient, and often uninvited. This is not a benign shift. It is the micro-erosion of sovereignty.

We live in an attention economy that thrives on our inability to say no. Every notification is a bid; every algorithm a persistent suitor. The modern dilemma is not a lack of access to information—it is the glut of unfiltered input, arriving faster than we can metabolise. In this context, *saying no to noise* is not simply a productivity tip. It is a spiritual act of self-defence.

What counts as "noise"? It is not merely the loud or the obnoxious. Noise is anything that fragments your presence, hijacks your agency, or obscures your values. It is the open-tab syndrome of modern consciousness—the feeling of being perennially mid-scroll, mid-thought, mid-life. And without intervention, it becomes the default setting.

To reclaim time and attention in this context is not to retreat into silence, but to *curate signal.* It is to distinguish between the urgent and the meaningful, the loud and the true. And this requires tools—not just willpower, but language, structure, and a philosophical lens that frames boundaries not as rejection, but as reverence.

Why Noise Dominates Modern Life

There is a reason we feel overwhelmed, even when ostensibly "doing nothing." In the last decade, neuroscientists have confirmed that our brains process digital inputs differently than they do analogue or embodied experiences. High-frequency, high-volume information triggers dopamine-rich anticipation loops, which keep us on the hook long after the content has been forgotten. The consequence? *A nervous system that confuses urgency with importance.*

The culture surrounding us does little to correct this. Hustle is valorised. Busyness is mistaken for relevance. The phrase "I'm so slammed" has become a badge of honour, not a signal of distress. This ambient glorification of overload makes it difficult to opt out without guilt or social friction. And so, we consent to distraction—passively, but repeatedly—until attention becomes a commodity we've unknowingly leased out.

The Moral Clarity of a Well-Placed No

To say no in this context is to honour your own architecture. It is to recognise that boundaries are not walls; they are membranes—porous, intelligent, and discerning. A "no" to digital noise is a "yes" to inner signal. But this requires conscious design.

It begins with language. Many of us know we need to unplug, but we lack the scripts to make that intention actionable. We don't know how to say:

"I don't check messages before 10am so I can be fully present when I do."

"This weekend is screen-free for me. If it's urgent, call me. Otherwise, I'll respond Monday."

"I'm intentionally protecting my mornings. Let's connect in the afternoon."

These are not evasions. They are declarations of design. Each one signals a commitment to rhythm, not reaction. And when spoken consistently, they don't just manage expectations; they model a new social norm—one in which clarity is more valued than constant availability.

Building Your Own 'No' Vocabulary

Crafting a personal lexicon of refusal is one of the most liberating mental exercises you can do. It reframes saying no not as scarcity, but as sovereignty. Consider the following approaches:

The Gentle Decline: "Thanks for the invitation—it means a lot. I'm keeping things really simple right now so I won't join, but I hope it's a beautiful gathering."

The Value Reframe: "I've found that constant group chats scatter my attention. I'm stepping back so I can show up more deeply elsewhere."

The Time Audit: "I'm looking closely at how I spend my mornings, and I've noticed early emails derail my focus. I'll be checking messages after noon going forward."

None of these require apology. They are not rejections of people—they are rejections of *default mode*. And in a hyper-stimulated culture, that alone is an act of quiet rebellion.

Designing Structural Boundaries for Attention

While scripts are essential, they are only as effective as the structures that support them. You cannot say no to digital noise if your environment screams yes. In this sense, your calendar, physical space, and digital interfaces are all part of your boundary architecture. And unlike reactive discipline, structural boundaries *work upstream*. They make desirable behaviours default, not dependent on moment-to-moment willpower.

Start with time. The philosopher José Ortega y Gasset once wrote, "Tell me to what you pay attention and I will tell you who you are." In the context of a noisy world, this becomes: *Design your day or someone else will.* The first and last 30 minutes of your waking hours are sacred neural terrain. They set tone and close loops. If you reach for your phone before your feet touch the ground, you've outsourced your mental agenda before your own voice has even emerged. Reclaiming these bookends of the day is not indulgent. It is infrastructural.

Create tech-free rituals that signal transition and sovereignty. A warm drink before screens. A handwritten note to yourself. A poem. Breath. Silence. These are not aesthetic flourishes. They are anchors. Rituals that train the nervous system to feel safe *without* stimulation are the antidote to what some neuroscientists call "anticipatory fatigue"—the mental weariness that comes from being always a swipe away from more.

Now turn to space. Your home, your workspace, even your phone screen—all of them are information landscapes. The fewer micro-decisions required to protect your attention, the stronger your inner signal becomes. Rearranging furniture, removing devices from the bedroom, even deleting a single app from your home screen can be a radical act of design. *Friction is not the enemy—unconscious access is.*

The Hidden Cost of Micro-Noise

We often tolerate small distractions because they feel inconsequential: the WhatsApp ping, the auto-playing YouTube sidebar, the impulse to check email during a conversation. But what we sacrifice in those moments is not just time—it's *cognitive coherence.* Research in neuropsychology shows that every interruption requires a "switch cost"—a measurable decline in performance and emotional presence that lingers long after the distraction is gone.

These switch costs accumulate. They're the reason a day filled with minor interruptions feels more exhausting than a day of deep focus. They're why multitasking doesn't just reduce productivity—it erodes the *quality of self* that shows up in any task. Saying no to noise, then, is not about efficiency. It is about *identity integrity.*

When you protect your attention, you are not just managing your tasks. You are stewarding your capacity to relate—first to yourself, then to others, and finally to the world. Without attention, there is no intimacy. No clarity. No real authorship. Just an ambient drift from notification to notification, in which days pass but meaning does not accumulate.

Grace, Not Grit

One of the most damaging myths of digital self-help is that boundaries are about willpower. They're not. Boundaries that rely on force are brittle. Boundaries that emerge from clarity are graceful. The more you know what matters, the easier it is to recognise what doesn't. And the easier it becomes to decline with kindness—both to yourself and to others.

This is where personal scripts and systems converge: not as mechanisms of restriction, but of expansion. You are not closing yourself off from the world. You are tuning yourself to it—choosing which frequencies nourish and which drain. And that discernment is not cold. It is sacred.

Saying no to noise allows your life to become porous again—not to interruption, but to beauty. You hear the birds. You feel your breath. You finish conversations. You remember books. You notice that moment at 3:27pm when the light hits the wall *just right* and everything pauses, briefly, into coherence. That's the signal you've been waiting for. But it can't find you through static.

Rehearsing Presence: The Practice of Mindful No

A powerful no is not a rejection of life—it's a conscious *yes* to the aspects of it that make you whole. Saying no to noise, then, is a philosophical posture as much as it is a practical one. It requires what might be called *mindful resistance*—the deliberate and ongoing practice of returning to what matters, again and again, with reverence.

This means you don't just say no once and expect the world to rearrange itself. You rehearse it. You design it into your day, your spaces, your relationships, your technologies. You make saying no not just a boundary but a *rhythm.* A drumbeat underneath the pace of your life that keeps you steady when everything else accelerates.

Rehearsing presence involves small but sacred disciplines. Turning off notifications is not just a setting—it is a ritual of return. Leaving your phone in another room during a meal is not merely an etiquette—it's a reclamation of relational sanctity. And logging off from a meeting five minutes early to breathe before the next one is not inefficiency—it is *integration.*

The wisdom traditions have long taught that silence is not empty. It is full of answers. But to hear those answers, we must first become *available* to them. This availability—mental, emotional, and spiritual—is what noise erodes. Reclaiming it is not about monastic withdrawal. It's about *participation with discernment.*

Becoming the Steward of Your Signal

Every time you check your phone reflexively, you're not just checking a message. You're *checking out* of yourself. You're deferring your inner authority to the most urgent stimulus. And you're reinforcing a feedback loop in which silence becomes uncomfortable and stimulus becomes default.

But when you begin to say no—gracefully, intentionally—you reverse the loop. You become the steward of your own signal. You start asking better questions: *Does this input deepen my presence or scatter it? Does it honour my priorities or hijack them? Is this mine to carry—or simply noise?*

This is the art. Not the rigidity of digital abstinence. Not the guilt of imperfection. But the *fluid competence* of a person who knows what their attention is worth—and treats it accordingly. In this way, saying no is not just a defence. It is a declaration: that you value clarity over chaos, depth over distraction, and reality over reaction.

Closing the Circuit

There is a moment, if you practise this long enough, when the noise recedes and something else arrives: *stillness, yes—but also signal.* An intuition. A knowing. A creative thread. A forgotten memory. A conversation with the self that's been waiting at the edge of interruption to be invited back in.

And in that moment, you realise that saying no to noise was never about deprivation. It was about *amplification.* Of meaning. Of soul. Of choice.

Because the world will always be loud. The question is: *Will you be listening to it, or to yourself?*

That's not a rhetorical flourish. That's a sacred decision. One made not just once, but daily. Hourly. Gently.

One *no* at a time.

Designing a Life That Doesn't Need Escapes

The most radical act of well-being in the digital age may not be a detox or a digital fast. It may be the quiet, steady commitment to architecting a life from which you do not constantly need to flee. In a world that sells escapism as self-care and distraction as normalcy, the true luxury is not a better app, but a better baseline—one of alignment, not addiction. This subchapter explores what it means to live in a way that renders the craving for constant digital relief obsolete. It offers not a critique of screens, but a deeper inquiry: *What are we designing our lives around—and why must we keep leaving them?*

The question is not whether we need breaks from modern life. That much is clear. What is at stake is what our need to escape is telling us about the systems we live inside—both externally and internally. If digital overuse is a symptom, then our solution must go beneath the surface. It must reimagine the very structures of our days, our work, our environments, and even our identities.

The Myth of Earned Rest

Much of modern culture operates on the assumption that rest must be earned—after productivity, after achievement, after exhaustion. This mindset is tightly wound with the logic of escapism. If rest is only allowed when we've pushed ourselves to the brink, then of course we will associate restoration with collapse, not consistency. Digital escapes become small rebellions: a scrolling session in the bathroom, a binge-watch marathon, a dopamine-fuelled detour. But when rest is reclaimed as a *right*—not a reward—then the need for escape softens. We are no longer fleeing a life we've built, but inhabiting one that sustains us by design.

The Architecture of Alignment

A life that doesn't require escapism is not built by accident. It is *designed*—deliberately, courageously, and often counter-culturally. It begins with a shift in design principles. Instead of asking, *What maximises output?* the better question becomes, *What supports alignment?* Alignment is not productivity. It is coherence between one's values, energy, attention, and environment. It is the sensation of living *from within*, not always chasing something beyond.

Designing such a life might involve unsexy, non-Instagrammable choices: protecting white space on your calendar, committing to analogue mornings, refusing work that violates your deeper principles. It might mean reworking your definition of success altogether—from external achievement to internal congruence. It is slow. It is often invisible. And it is the bedrock of true liberation.

Case Study: The Workspace that Heals

Consider the shift made by a design firm in Copenhagen that noticed its employees were increasingly distracted, burnt out, and addicted to micro-escapes during work hours. Rather than instituting another round of mindfulness training, leadership restructured the physical space and schedule of the office. They introduced "deep work blocks" with no notifications allowed, created technology-free "quiet corners" that mimicked library sanctuaries, and shortened meetings by default. The result was not just fewer distractions—it was fewer desires to escape at all. The environment, in other words, had been re-coded to reduce the need for relief.

This is not just about offices. It's about recognising that systems—home systems, relational systems, personal routines—can either foster fragmentation or facilitate coherence. Where there is coherence, the hunger to numb diminishes.

Moving From Coping to Creating

Many of us use digital distractions as coping mechanisms for emotional overload. And sometimes that is necessary. But a life built on coping alone becomes a flat existence—a constant negotiation between stress and sedation. The antidote is to shift from *coping* to *creating*. This doesn't mean more hustle or output. It means becoming a conscious designer of your hours, your rhythms, your rituals. It means reclaiming authorship over the sensory inputs you allow in, the conversations you engage with, and the expectations you set for yourself.

For example, instead of collapsing into YouTube at the end of a workday, what if your wind-down was a bath with candles and music that nourishes rather than numbs? Instead of reaching for your phone during a moment of boredom, what if your instinct was to stretch, breathe, or gaze out the window? These are micro-practices, yes—but they form a macro-narrative: *I live a life I want to be present for.*

The Psychology of Presence

At the heart of this redesign is presence—the ability to be where you are, as you are, without the compulsive itch to leave. Presence is not a spiritual abstraction; it is a nervous system skill. When your life is filled with unresolved tension, competing values, and over-scheduling, presence becomes intolerable. You will naturally seek out relief through scrolling, snacking, overworking, or numbing.

But when your systems are supportive—when you build a home that nurtures nervous system safety, a workflow that respects cognitive rhythm, and relationships that honour your emotional truth—presence becomes not only possible, but pleasurable. The craving to escape diminishes because you are no longer at war with your reality.

Practical Design Interventions

Audit your escape points: What times of day or contexts most drive you to flee? Map them. Don't moralise them—observe them. These are diagnostic signals, not failures.

Design for presence, not perfection: Your life doesn't need to look good—it needs to *feel* good. That means honouring body rhythms, building in micro-pauses, and creating buffers between activities.

Protect your emotional core: Build rituals that centre you—morning grounding, end-of-day reflection, weekly realignment. These are not indulgences; they are your psychological infrastructure.

Normalize sacred limits: Say no. Often. Not from scarcity, but from sovereignty. A well-boundaried life is one that contains enough space to breathe, digest, and re-centre.

Reframing Freedom

True freedom is not the ability to leave at will—it is the *absence of compulsion to leave at all.* In this sense, the most profound digital detox is not the one you schedule. It's the life you shape that doesn't require a detox in the first place. That life is built not through grand gestures, but through slow, consistent acts of self-honouring. Through boundaries that are less about restriction and more about reverence.

The goal is not to shame digital tools, but to render them optional. The goal is not to create a perfectly serene existence, but one that feels like it belongs to you. Where rest is not an escape. Where attention is not outsourced. Where your time—your very *being*—is no longer something you need to flee.

Because when your life is aligned, you don't need to escape it. You want to stay.

Chapter 9
Integration—Living a Detoxed Life

The true measure of transformation isn't how pristine we emerge from the ritual—but whether we live, steadily and consciously, the truths it revealed. Detox, as it's commonly framed, tends to be seen as a temporary pause—a sanctioned withdrawal from excess, a kind of moral timeout for modern indulgence. But look closer, and detox is no endpoint. It's a threshold. What matters more is what follows. And that's where this chapter plants its flag: in the terrain of integration. Not as some vague notion of balance, but as a daily rhythm—a lived recalibration—a new way of meeting the digital world with a grounded presence and a touch more reverence.

Contemporary life, to put it plainly, is built for backsliding. Screens and speed and overstimulation—they don't conspire against us so much as take advantage of what we've left unfortified. Often, those returning from a digital detox fall straight back into old grooves—not because of failure or lack of will, but because there's no scaffolding in place. A detox without deliberate design crumbles easily. Intention without infrastructure? It barely lasts the week. This chapter is about creating the kind of architecture—external and internal—that can support a detoxed life. A life in which attention is no longer a daily skirmish but a form of conscious stewardship.

Let's begin by rethinking what a digital detox is meant to achieve. It's not a permanent retreat from the modern world, clutching a journal in one hand and a candle in the other while notifications pile up somewhere beyond your reach. Nor is it about swearing off technology in some performative act of renunciation. Rather, it's an invitation to let detox evolve into a shift in cultural posture—a subtle, enduring reorientation. Integration, in this sense, is about taking the quiet clarity found in disconnection and threading it through our ordinary hours. It's about letting moments of stillness mature into values, letting those values grow into habits, and letting those habits inform the systems by which we live.

What follows are what we might call anchor practices—three daily touchpoints, not because you must, but because they help. They're not designed to optimise your output or give your mornings a 'glow-up.' They exist as stabilisers for the nervous system, markers of self-respect, reminders—often in the face of chaos—that your worth is not tethered to efficiency. Think of them like a compass for the soul: not to narrow your range, but to help you keep your bearings.

We also need to break apart the tired narrative of digital purity versus relapse. This all-or-nothing mindset—the one that's long plagued the wellness world—has no place here. Eat clean or you've failed. Meditate every day or don't bother. Quit your apps or be a hypocrite. But life rarely unfolds in binaries. Just as nutritional health depends on variety, not austerity, digital wellbeing thrives not on abstinence, but on intentionality. This chapter will guide you toward a more sustainable, deeply human way of engaging online—one that honours your work, your creativity, and your lived reality, without handing over your sovereignty.

Of course, lapses happen. Relapse, despite the stigma that clings to the word, is part of any true rhythm. Muscles tremble before they strengthen. Minds wander before they deepen. When your attention strays—or crashes altogether—it doesn't mean you've failed. It means you're in the process. The question is not how to avoid the lapse, but how to return. This section offers language and recovery rituals rooted in compassion, not shame. Tools, not penalties. Because each return is a chance to reinforce the path—not abandon it.

And then, we arrive at what might be called a redefinition of digital success. It's no longer about shaving down your screen time or reaching the mythical "inbox zero." It's about whether your inner life feels more luminous, more intact. To live a detoxed life isn't to run from the digital commons. It's to enter it consciously—with firm boundaries, clear tools, and systems that echo a life you no longer wish to delay. What you need, in the end, isn't more willpower. You need resonance.

The word *integration* has a gentle ring to it, doesn't it? As though it's the moment everything clicks into place. But real integration? It's far messier. It doesn't arrive on soft feet. It must be practised—deliberately, sometimes unglamorously, every day. It's the act of continuing what you remembered in stillness, not only when the world is hushed, but precisely when it's not—when the inbox demands and the algorithms sparkle and the pull to drift is stronger than ever.

To meet that moment, we need to shift from relying on sheer willpower to designing our lives more intelligently. Willpower has a romantic appeal, sure, but it's fleeting. It burns hot, then fizzles. Design, however—design endures. When your environment—your calendar, your home, your relationships—is shaped with care, it begins to do some of the heavy lifting. You don't have to keep remembering what to resist; the resistance has already been built into the blueprint. That's the pivot—from exhausting effort to thoughtful structure.

This applies everywhere: from the way you lay out your day to how your apps are grouped (or hidden), to how you handle social obligations. Is your evening device-free by design, or just by chance? Does your workspace nudge you towards stillness or scatter? Have you set clear lines around what digital input you consider essential—and have you truly granted yourself permission to ignore the rest? While this chapter won't prescribe your exact systems, it will offer a way of thinking—a methodology to build those systems in harmony with what matters most to *you*, rather than in response to the noisy defaults of a distracted culture.

Alongside this outer framework, we must also tend to the internal scaffolding: identity. Lasting change, more often than not, arises from the quiet conviction of who we believe we are. If you still carry the story that you're someone "bad at boundaries," no amount of digital hygiene will stick. But if you begin to inhabit the self-image of someone who treats their attention as sacred, then new behaviours—no matter how small—start to feel less like effort, and more like expression. A detoxed life, in this light, isn't just a shift in habits. It's a redefinition of self.

And we cannot speak of integration without speaking of others. For all its inward focus, this is not solitary work. Detox might be a private act, but reintegration flourishes in the shared field of relationship. When the people around you perform distractedness, glorify burnout, and confuse constant connection for intimacy, it takes real clarity to do things differently. We'll explore how to nurture micro-communities—pockets of kinship grounded not in shared platforms, but in shared presence. These are not merely people who unplug. They are those who remember how to be plugged into *themselves*.

At its core, integration is a return. Not a return to business as usual, nor to the norms that made you need a detox in the first place—but a return to what's essential. To the heartbeat beneath the to-do list. To the clarity that lives beyond the noise. To the part of you that no longer confuses stimulation for meaning or believes that rest must be earned. What follows in this chapter is your toolkit for that return—grounded, lived, and quietly revolutionary.

There is no single path forward. But there is, perhaps, a universal condition for success: that you begin to place more trust in yourself than in your devices. Not because technology is the villain—but because it was never built to hold your wholeness. That part, the sacred part, is yours to tend.

Let this chapter not feel like an ending. Let it be a threshold. A beginning of sorts. Where detox is no longer a corrective, but simply a remembering—a way of being that no longer feels like resistance, but like coming home.

From Cleanse to Culture: Designing a Soul-Aligned Digital Life

Detox, by definition, implies removal—of toxins, excesses, or disturbances. It is the beginning, not the end. And yet, for many, a digital detox is treated like a reset button: a temporary reprieve, a breath of relief before diving back into the same frenzied currents. What is rarely asked is this: *What comes after the cleanse?* The real transformation begins when detox becomes design—when the architecture of your digital life is shaped not by default, but by deliberate cultural values. A digital detox without cultural integration is a silence without a new song.

The modern digital ecosystem, designed for velocity and volume, seduces users into lives of constant reaction. In such an environment, detox alone risks becoming another checkbox in the productivity matrix—a personal improvement task that paradoxically reinforces the very compulsion it seeks to unravel. To move beyond this, one must reimagine detox as a gateway to culture: the intentional creation of rituals, rhythms, and relationships that support a coherent, soul-aligned way of living with technology.

Culture in this context does not mean the external trappings of digital sophistication—minimalist interfaces, curated feeds, or app-blockers. It means an embodied ethic: how we move through digital spaces with integrity, discernment, and self-possession. This is not about using less. It is about using differently.

The Myth of Re-entry

One of the most overlooked challenges of digital detoxing is what happens *after*. The return. The re-entry. Many people treat a detox like a cleanse from sugar or caffeine—an extreme abstinence followed by a gradual reintroduction. But with digital tools, there is no moderate reintroduction without cultural scaffolding. The platforms do not re-enter gently. They flood. Algorithms do not whisper; they shout. Without intentional guardrails, relapse is not just likely—it is architected.

And so, detox must be followed not by return, but by redesign. The question becomes: *What do I want my digital culture to reflect about what I value most deeply?* This is where the shift from cleanse to culture begins.

From Subtraction to Substitution

Minimalism often fails as a long-term solution because it privileges absence over essence. Removing distractions is not the same as cultivating depth. Instead of simply subtracting digital stimuli, we must substitute them with meaning. Replace the scroll with a sacred ritual. Swap the reflexive refresh for a deliberate practice. Turn the phone face-down and lift your own gaze. Ask not only *what am I removing?* but *what am I returning to?*

This transition requires anchoring practices—daily rituals that stabilise the nervous system and reinforce intentionality. These are not merely "habits" in the self-help sense. They are cultural gestures: micro-expressions of a larger inner commitment. Examples include morning breathwork before checking messages, a candle-lit journaling session at dusk, or even a weekly digital Sabbath that functions less as withdrawal and more as reverence.

The Ethics of Attention

Culture is not neutral. Every system we participate in shapes our moral landscape. What we attend to becomes what we value. In a soul-aligned digital life, attention is not a currency—it is a consecration. This reframing invites a moral dimension to our scrolling, clicking, and consuming. Are we honouring the sacredness of our attention? Or are we leaking it into voids designed for monetisation?

To shift from cleanse to culture, one must treat attention as an ethical act. This means curating not only what we consume, but also what we contribute. It means refusing to amplify outrage for the sake of engagement. It means pausing before posting—not to polish a persona, but to ensure alignment with deeper truths. Culture is not what we perform publicly—it is what we protect privately.

Relapse and Renewal

A soul-aligned digital culture is not immune to setbacks. You will scroll unconsciously again. You will binge-watch. You will reach for the device when silence grows uncomfortable. But these moments are not failures—they are invitations. Every relapse is a return path to renewal, if met with awareness rather than shame.

The goal is not perfection, but rhythm. A culture that welcomes recalibration. This requires a compassionate inner stance—one that understands that old neural pathways take time to rewire. Design systems that forgive. Build practices that recover rather than punish. Treat relapse not as erosion, but as erosion's counterpoint: the sculpting of a more sustainable shape.

Living the Question

To shift from detox to design is to live a question: *What kind of digital world am I shaping through my smallest choices?* When this question becomes the heartbeat of your daily interactions—when it informs how you wake, how you pause, how you connect—then detox has truly become culture.

This transition does not happen in a single day. It is cultivated in layers—through decisions made in the first 30 minutes of the morning, through moments of pause before reaction, through saying no when noise tries to reassert itself as necessity. It is the slow, dignified building of a world in which your nervous system feels at home.

From cleanse to culture is not a task. It is a remembering. Of what you once knew before the noise. Of what you still carry underneath the scroll.

And of what you are called to create—not just for yourself, but for the digital civilisation we are all complicit in crafting.

Anchor Practices for Long-Term Balance

Three Daily Rituals to Regulate the Nervous System and Sustain Inner Clarity

Modern life moves at a velocity that the human nervous system did not evolve to endure. Screens flicker before our eyes from the moment we wake. Notifications punctuate the rhythm of our days like artificial thunder. And beneath it all runs a quiet but potent question: can we keep living like this without consequence?

The answer is no. But the antidote is not an escape from the world—it's the design of one's inner architecture. What the nervous system requires isn't more apps to track wellness, but fewer moments of fragmentation. It needs rhythm, not speed. Presence, not performance. It needs anchors—simple, deliberate practices that tether the psyche back to safety and coherence. These anchors are not luxuries or lifestyle hacks. They are physiological necessities. And when honoured daily, they can return us to ourselves.

This article introduces three such anchor practices—each brief, accessible, and neurologically grounded. When integrated consistently, they offer more than stress relief. They establish a foundation for a life lived from within.

1. Morning Stillness: The Art of Deliberate Arrival

Before emails are opened, before news is absorbed, and long before the world is allowed to shape the tone of the day, there must be a pause. Morning stillness is not about achieving enlightenment. It's about allowing the body and mind to re-enter consciousness without assault.

The first thirty minutes after waking are uniquely neuroplastic. The brain is in a theta-alpha state—a bridge between subconscious imagery and conscious processing. Input during this time imprints deeply. If the day begins with urgency, interruption, or external stimulation, the nervous system is primed for reactivity rather than agency.

A sustainable anchor practice: sit in silence for five minutes upon waking. No phone. No mental to-do lists. Simply sit. Feel your breath moving. Let your awareness drop into your body like a stone into still water. This practice may seem negligible—but physiologically, it reorients the system toward presence. What begins as five minutes often expands organically into meditation, journaling, or breathwork. But the seed is stillness.

2. Midday Breath Reset: Regulating from Within

The human stress response is elegant in its design, but tragic in its misuse. We were built for short bursts of stress followed by restoration. What we endure now is continuous activation without interruption. The result is nervous systems stuck in sympathetic overdrive—anxious, fatigued, ungrounded.

But the breath offers a direct, sovereign route to regulation. Unlike heart rate or digestion, breath is a bridge between voluntary and involuntary systems. When we change how we breathe, we send real-time updates to the brain about our state of safety.

One anchor practice: the 4-7-8 technique. Inhale through the nose for four seconds. Hold for seven. Exhale through the mouth for eight. Repeat for four cycles. This ratio stimulates the vagus nerve and shifts the system from fight-or-flight into parasympathetic calm. It's efficient. It's elegant. And done once mid-morning and once mid-afternoon, it can reset an entire internal rhythm—without apps, screens, or effort.

3. Evening Integration: Conscious Closure

How we end the day is as crucial as how we begin it. Sleep is not a switch—it is a physiological descent. But for many, bedtime is preceded by scrolling, stimulation, and unresolved emotions. The body may be horizontal, but the mind is still online.

Evening integration means creating a closing ritual that signals safety and completion to the nervous system. This is not about perfection—it's about transition.

A powerful anchor practice is reflective journaling. But this is not a diary entry. It is a brief, structured process of emotional integration. Ask three questions: What did I feel today? What did I need but not receive? What am I ready to release?

This practice metabolises the day's emotional content. It prevents the mind from recycling incomplete loops during sleep. Neuroscientifically, it allows the prefrontal cortex to return to balance, supporting deep rest and memory consolidation.

For those who resist journaling, an alternative: fifteen minutes of screen-free, low-stimulation activity before bed—reading a physical book, stretching slowly, or simply sitting by candlelight. What matters is that the external world is gently closed, and the inner world acknowledged.

From Ritual to Rhythm: Why These Three Matter

Individually, these practices are modest. But their power lies in consistency, not complexity. They are non-negotiables not because of dogma, but because the nervous system thrives on rhythm. These anchors are not about discipline—they're about devotion to one's own aliveness.

The common temptation is to treat these practices as tools to 'fix' overwhelm. But that frames the human nervous system as a problem. A healthier frame: these anchors are love letters to the body. They are reminders that regulation is not a luxury—it is a biological right.

The future belongs not to those who out-hustle others, but to those who can remain centred amidst noise. In a culture addicted to the next ping, the real rebellion is breath. The real revolution is stillness. And the real transformation begins not in extraordinary effort, but in ordinary ritual, done daily, with care.

Digital Hygiene vs. Digital Abstinence: Crafting a Sustainable Relationship with the Screen

It's tempting to treat digital excess the same way we treat sugar, caffeine, or alcohol: with detoxes, fasts, and firm lines drawn in the sand. The allure of a hard reset appeals to our craving for control, for purity, for a clean break from the overstimulation we know is eroding our mental and emotional balance. But here's the quiet truth most productivity evangelists and wellness influencers overlook: what we often need is not a total renunciation of technology, but a wiser way to live with it. Not abstinence, but hygiene. Not a purge, but a practice.

We don't demonise books when we read too much. We don't abandon food when we overeat. Yet when it comes to our digital lives, the conversation still tilts towards binary extremes—on or off, plugged in or purged, dopamine-flooded or digitally sober. This dichotomy, while emotionally satisfying in the short term, rarely holds up to the complexities of modern life. Most people cannot afford a permanent digital disappearance. Nor should they have to. What we need instead is a philosophy of use that matches the depth and dimensionality of the tools themselves.

Digital hygiene—a term gaining quiet traction among psychologists, educators, and mindfulness practitioners—does not seek to eliminate screens from our lives. It seeks to *recontextualise* them. To treat digital inputs with the same intentionality we might bring to our diet, our relationships, or our finances. Hygiene is ongoing. It is imperfect. It is flexible. And unlike abstinence, which implies a one-size-fits-all morality, hygiene adapts itself to context, to season, and to individual need.

To understand why digital hygiene matters, we must first acknowledge that our nervous systems were not designed for the constant cognitive pinging that now punctuates every hour. Push notifications, infinite scrolls, algorithmic recommendations, and attention-hijacking design cues don't just compete for our time—they colonise our inner space. Over time, they begin to shape what we notice, what we value, and how we feel about ourselves. Digital abstinence, while useful as a temporary reset, often fails to address the root issue: our lack of conscious frameworks for sustained, empowered engagement.

The essence of digital hygiene is *curation over consumption.* It's the art of choosing what enters your awareness, and when. It's knowing that you don't have to check your email first thing in the morning—not because it's inherently evil, but because your nervous system deserves sovereignty. It's understanding that you can watch a documentary on your tablet at night and still have a tech-respectful relationship, because you chose it consciously, rather than being dragged by habit.

Let's be clear: abstinence has its place. There are moments—crucial, sacred moments—when full disconnection is both a necessary medicine and a spiritual act. Retreats, Sabbaths, deep creative immersion, grief periods—these are times when the silence of no-screen life can be deeply healing. But treating abstinence as a default mode rather than a deliberate exception sets most of us up for failure, guilt, and cyclical bingeing.

Consider a parallel from nutrition. No one would argue that fasting has benefits. But we also know that long-term wellness depends more on what we consistently eat than what we occasionally avoid. The same is true of digital life. A three-day fast from your phone may be revelatory, but if it's followed by weeks of unconscious bingeing, the long-term effect may be negligible. Hygiene asks: *What are your daily rituals of care? What does your media diet nourish? When do you check in with your emotional state before logging on?*

This approach has implications beyond personal wellbeing. Digital hygiene is also a cultural stance. It challenges the economy of attention, the commodification of time, and the silent assumption that faster is better and more is meaningful. It says: I refuse to be available 24/7, not out of rebellion, but out of reverence. I choose presence over pace, not because I'm weak, but because I value depth over dopamine.

The conversation must also include compassion. We are not failures when we scroll longer than intended. We are not weak when we reach for the screen out of boredom, loneliness, or overwhelm. Hygiene allows room for humanity. It recognises that our tech use is often a symptom of unmet emotional needs—and that healing doesn't come through shaming, but through subtle recalibrations over time.

In the chapters ahead, readers are invited to experiment with practical frameworks for digital hygiene—daily boundary rituals, content audits, intentional consumption prompts, and nervous-system check-ins. These are not meant to be rigid rules, but supportive companions in the ongoing dance between self and screen. The goal is not perfection. It is congruence.

Ultimately, digital hygiene isn't about becoming someone who never scrolls. It's about becoming someone who knows why they're scrolling, when to stop, and how to return to the stillness within. In a culture that confuses stimulation with aliveness, this clarity is a quiet form of power. And like all true forms of power, it begins not with control, but with care.

Relapse as Part of the Rhythm: A Compassionate Architecture for Sustainable Digital Healing

There is a deeply entrenched narrative in modern culture that equates relapse with failure. Whether in health, productivity, or attention management, a single lapse is often framed as undoing all prior progress—as if healing were a one-way street paved only with flawless execution. This mindset is particularly destructive when applied to the nuanced terrain of digital wellness. The myth that a single scroll, binge, or lapse in boundary somehow negates an entire practice of intentionality is not only inaccurate—it is psychologically counterproductive. In reality, relapse is not an interruption of the process. It is part of it. A rhythm. A return. A reminder that we are not machines optimising an operating system, but human beings learning to live in right relation with an overwhelmingly digital world.

To understand why relapse must be normalised—not pathologised—we must first reject the perfectionist lens through which most digital detox narratives are filtered. The prevailing model often mirrors dietary cleanse culture: binary, rigid, and ultimately unsustainable. A person commits to a 21-day detox, perhaps abstains from screens for a weekend retreat, and then reenters daily life expecting to be "cured." But when the tides of dopamine crash back through familiar loops—when late-night scrolling creeps in or inbox overload returns—it feels like backsliding. This reaction is built on a flawed premise: that digital clarity is a destination, not a discipline. In truth, digital harmony is cyclical. And just as the body breathes, digests, and sleeps in rhythms, so too does the psyche require oscillations between overstimulation and rebalancing.

Neuroscience supports this. The same circuits in the brain that learn new habits—via neuroplasticity—also unlearn them through the same mechanism of repetition. Setbacks are not the erasure of progress but moments of recalibration. They highlight unaddressed emotional cues or environmental stressors. Perhaps your digital relapse coincided with a period of emotional depletion. Perhaps it was social isolation. Or sheer exhaustion. These are not signs of failure. They are invitations to listen more closely.

This is why compassion must be built into the architecture of any meaningful digital reset. Without it, relapse becomes a shame trigger. And shame, as Brené Brown has powerfully argued, is a poor catalyst for sustainable change. A relapse is not a moral failing. It is a diagnostic flare. The key question is not "Why did I fail?" but "What need was I trying to meet?" This shift—from judgment to inquiry—creates the psychological spaciousness needed for growth.

Recovery tools must be designed with this nuance in mind. One powerful framework is the *relapse reflection ritual.* Rather than reacting with guilt, create a dedicated space—weekly or monthly—where you examine your patterns with gentleness. Use prompts such as:

What did I seek in that moment of disconnection?

What emotion preceded my return to the feed?

What boundary, if strengthened, could have better supported me?

This ritual reframes relapse as data. It turns the spotlight not on self-discipline, but on self-knowledge.

Equally vital is the reorientation of relapse duration. It is not the slip that defines the trajectory, but the return. A single evening lost in YouTube does not negate a month of clarity. What matters is how quickly, and how consciously, you come back. One of the most elegant psychological insights of our time is *cognitive flexibility*—the ability to pivot with grace. Not to prevent disruption, but to recover from it with intelligence.

To integrate this, consider building what I call *return anchors*. These are personal practices that require minimal effort but signal a psychological re-entry into intentional digital presence. It could be something as small as lighting a candle before logging on, closing your eyes for thirty seconds before checking your inbox, or taking a single conscious breath before unlocking your phone. These micro-rituals interrupt automaticity. They replace reactivity with rhythm.

Equally, we must recognise the cultural pressures that compound relapse. In a world where availability is mistaken for accountability, stepping away from digital demands often invites subtle (or not-so-subtle) forms of guilt or social friction. To relapse into hyperconnection can feel like a surrender to normativity—a giving in to what the world expects. And this, too, deserves compassion. We are not just battling personal habits. We are resisting systemic pressures that commodify attention, reward performative productivity, and punish stillness.

This is where soul-centred recovery diverges from conventional digital detox dogma. It is not about returning to an ideal state. It is about returning to *yourself.* Again and again. With softness. With sovereignty. With the conviction that digital relapse is not the antithesis of progress, but part of the rhythm of remembering what matters.

The Soul-Centred Way Forward

There is a quiet revolution underway. Beneath the clickbait headlines, algorithmic noise, and optimisation imperatives lies a growing hunger for something radically simple yet deeply subversive: the right to live on one's own terms. In a world that equates busyness with value and visibility with worth, choosing to define success by inner alignment rather than outer applause can feel almost rebellious. Yet this is precisely what the soul-centred path demands. It is not a lifestyle trend or wellness fad—it is a philosophical reorientation, a deliberate act of remembering what it means to be fully human in an age that constantly urges us to be something else.

The modern self is a curated entity. Every scroll invites comparison, every app nudges performance, and every notification reaffirms the notion that to matter is to be productive, responsive, and digitally present. Against this backdrop, the soul is not easily heard. It whispers—not in metrics, milestones, or motion, but in moments of quiet coherence. The soul doesn't shout for followers or demand a platform. It waits. It watches. And it wonders if you'll pause long enough to listen.

To walk the soul-centred path is to replace the question "What should I be doing?" with "What feels deeply right?" It is to move from optimisation to orientation—not what gets you the most done, but what brings you most alive. The soul is not concerned with inbox zero or quarterly KPIs. It's not tracking engagement rates. It's asking better questions: *Does this nourish me? Does this cost my peace? Is this a true yes, or a performative one?*

This reframing isn't indulgent—it's intelligent. We are not machines to be maximised. The nervous system, the emotional body, the imaginative mind—none of these thrive under perpetual acceleration. What they crave is rhythm, rest, resonance. And yet, so many of us live as though the only path to legitimacy is through output. The consequence is a kind of spiritual malnutrition: overfed on stimulation, starved of meaning.

Reclaiming success on soul terms requires courage. It means interrogating the scripts handed to us: that ambition must be loud, that stillness is laziness, that we owe the world our constant availability. It means moving from a life of achievement to a life of attunement—one where success is not how much you do, but how aligned you are while doing it. This isn't about abandoning responsibility or ambition. It's about redefining them. Responsibility, in this context, begins with the self: to stay rooted, to protect your clarity, to honour your rhythm. Ambition becomes less about acquisition and more about alignment. What if the most powerful thing you could build is not a brand, but an inner life that can't be shaken?

None of this is easy. It asks for discernment in a world of distraction. It invites depth in a culture of surfaces. It demands patience when immediacy is celebrated. But those who walk this path report something rare: a sense of peace not contingent on performance. A confidence not built on metrics. A joy that does not need to be photographed to be real.

The soul-centred way forward is not a retreat from modernity, but a reclaiming of autonomy within it. It means designing a life not around avoidance of pain or the pursuit of perfection, but around the pursuit of coherence. The goal is not to escape the world, but to show up to it so fully, so congruently, that your very presence is its own form of protest—a declaration that *this is what wholeness looks like.*

To live this way is to trade urgency for agency. It is to make peace with being unseen by the algorithms if it means being seen by yourself. It is to measure progress not by speed, but by alignment. Not by growth charts, but by soul whispers that say: *this is the way.*

Living from the soul is not about perpetual harmony or a life devoid of conflict. It is about integrity—a fidelity to one's deepest knowing, even when that knowing challenges cultural expectations or professional norms. For many, this path begins with disillusionment: with the burnout that accolades can't soothe, with the hollowness of applause that fades too quickly, with the ache that remains even after every box has been ticked. These moments of reckoning aren't failures. They are invitations—portals through which we are asked to shift from performance to presence.

Presence, in this context, is not passive. It is rigorous. It requires attention, discernment, and often uncomfortable honesty. To be soul-centred is to know your yes and your no—not reactively, but reverently. It means noticing when you are choosing out of fear of disapproval rather than from alignment. It means noticing how your body feels after a decision. The nervous system becomes a compass. Your breath becomes a barometer. Your inner silence becomes the final counsel.

But how do we sustain this path in a world that profits from our distraction? We must build structures that honour our soul rather than sabotage it. This includes boundary-setting as a sacred act. Not all access is earned. Not all invitations require acceptance. Just as a physical space can be designed for calm—through lighting, scent, or order—our calendar, our inbox, our feed must be curated as extensions of our values. If the soul is to speak, it needs quiet. If it is to guide, it needs space.

It also means rethinking time. The soul does not rush. Its logic is cyclical, not linear. There are seasons of emergence and seasons of dormancy. To live soul-centred is to release the tyranny of constant productivity and honour the legitimacy of stillness, gestation, and retreat. Not every hour must be monetised. Not every season must be maximised. Sometimes the most radical thing we can do is to rest—not as recovery from exhaustion, but as an act of resistance against a culture that equates worth with output.

And yet, the soul does not ask for perfection. It asks for honesty. There will be relapse. There will be moments where we once again find ourselves chasing validation, scrolling to soothe, saying yes when we mean no. The soul-centred way accounts for this. It offers gentleness, not guilt. It reframes setbacks as signals—not of failure, but of disconnection. Each return to self is a victory. Each pause for breath, a recalibration. Each choice for alignment, a renewal of vows.

The tools are subtle but potent. A morning in silence. An evening walk without earbuds. A refusal to reply immediately. A handwritten note instead of a comment. A Sabbath for the senses. These are not acts of nostalgia. They are design choices for a life that resists fragmentation. They anchor the sacred in the ordinary and remind us that soul work is not separate from life—it is the deeper dimension of it.

This path also widens our definition of joy. No longer is joy merely the high, the event, the milestone. Joy becomes the quiet coherence of living in alignment. It's the lightness of not betraying yourself. The exhale of knowing you said what needed to be said. The contentment that lingers not because of what you achieved, but because of how you showed up.

Ultimately, to live a soul-centred life is not to escape the digital age, but to engage it differently. It is not about banishing technology, but about mastering our relationship to it so that it becomes a tool, not a tyrant. This approach requires precision—not just about what we eliminate, but what we elevate. Which interactions nourish you?

Which platforms reflect your values? Which rituals return you to yourself? The aim is not to be anti-digital, but to be pro-human. To be aligned in such a way that your online presence is an extension—not an erosion—of your inner coherence.

This redefinition of success—rooted in congruence rather than conquest—demands a new metric system. Not followers, but fulfilment. Not likes, but alignment. Not optimisation, but embodiment. This shift is not a rejection of ambition, but a reorientation of it. A soul-centred person still builds, still contributes, still dreams—but with the awareness that the manner in which they create is as important as the outcome itself.

Clarity, then, is no longer a product of data alone. It is born of stillness. It arises in the moments when we stop trying to fix, hack, or improve ourselves long enough to listen to what is already true. In this stillness, the noise falls away and something more durable emerges: self-trust. And from self-trust, a new kind of confidence takes root—one that does not demand performance, but presence; not curation, but coherence.

The soul-centred way forward is not about becoming someone else. It is about unbecoming what never belonged. It is the quiet, brave act of coming home to yourself and deciding—every day, in small, sacred ways—to live from that place. This is the future of wellbeing in a wired world: not another app, not another metric, but a return to the interior—a re-enchantment of the self as the most reliable compass we have.

This chapter, and this book, do not end with a grand solution because the soul does not operate in conclusions. It continues in questions, in daily rituals, in honest pauses, and in the tender work of remembering what matters. You do not need more time. You need more alignment. You do not need to be more. You need to be here. Fully. Simply. Soulfully. That is not a retreat. It is a revolution.

Conclusion
The Reclaimed Self

There comes a peculiar hush—subtle, almost imperceptible—when the screen fades to black, the endless chime of alerts silences, and something unfamiliar takes hold. It's not quite peace, not yet. More like a disquieting stillness that asks more of you than noise ever did. In the absence of prompts and pings, you're left with the raw material of self: breath, sensation, memory, presence. And from that stark, unmediated space arises a question not of what's next, but what's now. What's here?

This chapter doesn't aim to revisit lessons or tie a tidy bow around the detox just endured. It's not a victory lap, nor a digest of takeaways. Think of it instead as a threshold. A reflective pause, not to be filled with yet more doing, but to invite a deeper reckoning: With all you now know, where will you place your attention?

In the glare of modern life, for all its connectivity and cleverness, we've bartered meaning for momentum. We've confused access with agency, noise with importance, and speed with closeness. Intimacy has been supplanted by immediacy; the inner world, once sacred, has been made searchable, commodified, and gamified. But abstinence alone—no matter how committed—is not redemption. Detox only begins the work. The deeper, more quietly radical task is integration: the art of building a life so in tune, so intact, that the urge to escape it gradually dissolves.

To reclaim one's life is not to enforce rigid control over every click and scroll, nor to demand perfection in our digital choices. It is, rather, to stand in reverence for one's own time and attention. And reverence is not brittle. It doesn't shatter under distraction or relapse. It endures. It returns—again and again—to a centre that remembers. Like breath. Like dusk. Like prayer.

And so, this chapter begins there—with rhythm. Not as poetic flourish, but as practical guide. The rituals offered here—perhaps a morning check-in, an evening buffer, or a boundary honoured gently but firmly—are not new strategies in productivity. They are, at heart, invitations to inhabit your own presence more fully. To reclaim your sovereignty. To become less seduced by digital glitter, and more anchored in what does not blink away.

The soul—yes, let's use the word, as unfashionable as it may sound—has never cared about the number of browser tabs, the efficiency of a routine, or the mythical ideal of an empty inbox. The soul, if it speaks at all, asks gentler, stranger things. Are you here? Are you faithful to what matters? Have you remembered the shape of yourself without the world's noise?

There's a certain pressure, particularly at the close of any self-exploration, to declare the birth of a new, better self. A kind of psychological rebrand—as if identity were something you could download. But in truth, transformation rarely looks like becoming. More often, it is an uncovering. The self worth reclaiming is not a perfected version waiting in the future. It is the self that's been beneath the flickering feed all along—the one that remembers stillness, that trusts sensation, that knows how to discern without a prompt.

This is not a path to flawlessness. This is a commitment to noticing—to recognising when your focus starts to slip into performance, when your attention veers toward comparison, when your boundaries thin. And then, gently, returning. The lines we draw around our time and energy need not be fortresses—they can be forms of devotion. Acts of care. Guardrails that hold us steady, not shut us off.

Protecting your nervous system—treating it as something sacred, as you would a sleeping child—is not indulgence. It is integrity. And with that integrity, you begin to shape a life that no longer needs digital anaesthesia to feel bearable.

There's no list at the end of this journey. Only a single, solid truth: the real world—your real life—was never hidden behind a screen. It was waiting inside you. And that is not sentimental fluff. It is neurological. It is emotional. It is existential. And it's waiting for you to remember.

So, now, at this quiet juncture, you're not being asked to finish anything. You're being invited to begin again. With each swipe, tap, or glance, to choose—perhaps imperfectly, but consciously. That is the point. Not mastery. Not certainty. Just the humility and the courage to ask, again and again:

What is worthy of my attention now?

This Closing Reflection Is Less a Bow-Tied Summary and More a Soul Invocation

Beyond Completion – The Invitation to Begin Again

There are endings that tie things neatly. This is not one of them.

In the landscape of digital detox, many readers seek a checklist, a wrap-up, a final prescription that says, "You've done enough." But such closures are illusions. This book was never a map to mastery. It was a mirror—and the final chapter is not a door shutting behind you, but a breath before a deeper threshold. The real transformation begins not when the screen dims, but when the self reawakens.

We are living in a time that celebrates noise, novelty, and notification. The nervous system is constantly asked to stretch beyond what it was evolutionarily designed to handle. We scroll through outrage, inspiration, envy, and absurdity—all within minutes—yet rarely pause to metabolise the emotional residue these fragments leave behind. What gets sacrificed in the process is not just stillness, but selfhood. The cost is not simply time—it is attention, and attention is the currency of consciousness.

To reach the end of a digital detox journey, then, is not to reach a point of perfection, nor even balance. It is to finally see the architecture of our modern lives clearly enough to choose again—intentionally, tenderly, even reverently. The final invitation is not to optimise your relationship with your phone, but to re-orient your relationship with yourself.

And that begins with a reckoning.

What have we been giving our attention to—and at what cost?

This is not a moral inquiry. It is an existential one. Because beneath the algorithms, beyond the productivity hacks, and outside the glow of curated lives lies a quieter question waiting for a listener: *What matters to you now?*

Reclamation is not a single act. It is a daily, hourly, moment-by-moment return. Return to breath. To body. To being. And it is in this return that the digital fades and the real world—*the inner world*—comes into view again. Not the projected self, but the felt one. Not the life we perform, but the life we inhabit.

This isn't about becoming perfect. It's about becoming present.

The Sacred Act of Choosing Again

We have been taught to fear silence—not because silence is dangerous, but because it is honest. In its spaciousness, there is no distraction to shield us from the subtle dissonances within: the tight jaw that speaks of unspoken frustration, the restless scroll that masks a quiet grief, the flurry of busyness that hides the ache of disconnection. When the noise subsides, what remains is the sound of our own unmet selfhood.

And yet, this is precisely where reconnection begins.

To reclaim oneself in a digital age is not to demonise technology—it is to de-automate our participation in it. To disrupt the trance of default. To realise that every click, every swipe, every scroll is not benign, but directional. Each micro-action reinforces a certain version of reality. The algorithms don't just learn what we like. They teach us who to be.

This is why the detox cannot end with abstinence. The work is not just to remove noise, but to develop discernment. It is to craft a new grammar of attention—one that does not conflate visibility with value, reaction with truth, or speed with importance. Attention, in its purest form, is a form of devotion. Where we place it determines not only what we see, but who we become.

This final chapter is not here to summarise. It is here to consecrate. To remind you that this has never been about logging off for good. It has been about learning to log back into your body, your breath, your inner knowing. The world behind the screen may offer information, amusement, escape. But the world within you offers something else entirely: wisdom. Alignment. Meaning.

Let this be a sacred interruption. A full-body pause. Not to retreat from the digital, but to re-enter it differently—anchored, aware, awake. Let the systems of your life begin to reflect the integrity of your values. Let your environment—physical and digital—become an ally, not an adversary. Let your rituals of attention be as intentional as your rituals of care.

And let the final question linger like incense in the room after the bell has rung: *What will you now choose to give your attention to?*

Because in the end, the real world was never behind the screen—it was always within.

About the Author

Grace Fields is a celebrated voice in the world of personal transformation, known for weaving psychological insight with soulful wisdom to help readers reclaim joy, clarity, and inner peace. With a background in positive psychology and a deep-rooted passion for mindful living, Grace has made it her mission to guide others toward a more intentional and meaningful life—one grounded not in noise or urgency, but in stillness, gratitude, and authentic connection.

Her previous bestselling works, The Science and Secrets of Lasting Happiness, The Science of Sleep: Unlocking the Secrets to Restful Nights, and Cultivating Happiness Through Minimalism: Finding Happiness Through Simplicity, have earned her a loyal readership across the globe. Each book serves as a beacon for those seeking to untangle from modern overwhelm and rediscover the beauty in life's simplest truths.

In her latest work, Digital Detox for the Soul: A 21-Day Mental Cleanse, Grace offers more than just a guide to unplugging—she offers a pathway to awakening. Drawing on neuropsychology, ancient traditions, and her own lived experience, she delivers a profound invitation: to reset not just our digital habits, but our relationship with time, presence, and self.

Grace is also a sought-after speaker and advocate for mindfulness, regularly hosting workshops and retreats that empower individuals to create lives rich with purpose and emotional well-being. Her work continues to inspire a growing movement of readers to slow down, look inward, and live with clarity, courage, and joy.

www.ingramcontent.com/pod-product-compliance
Lightning Source LLC
Chambersburg PA
CBHW031344230926
51848CB00002B/385